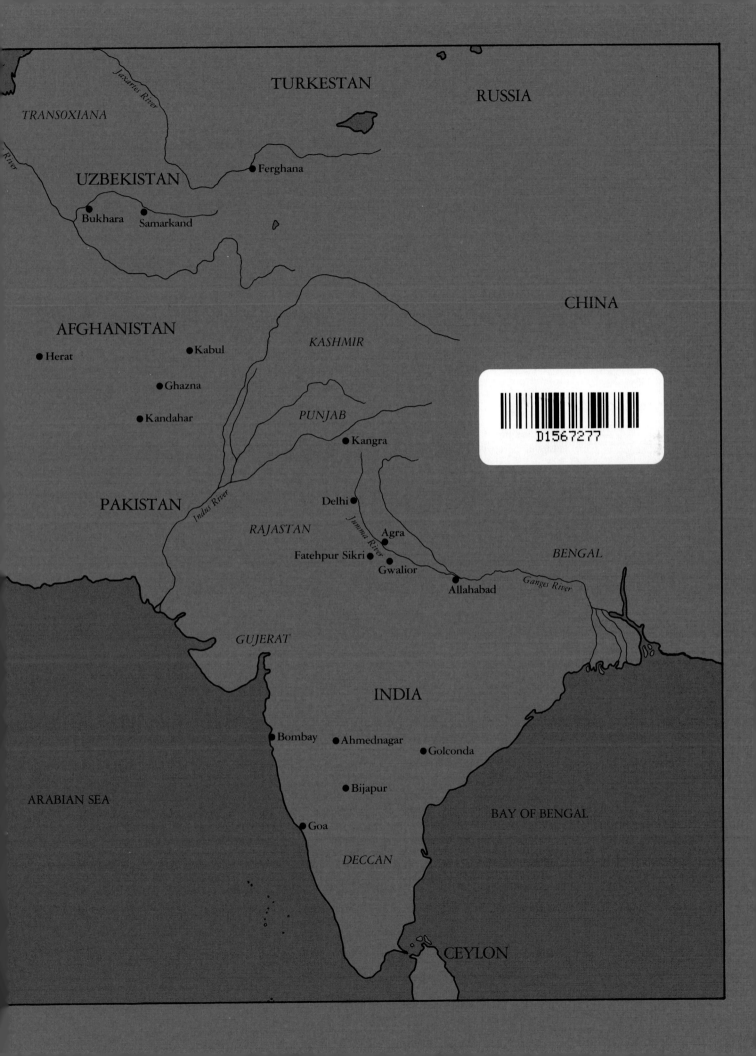

The Brush of the Masters: Drawings from Iran and India

Esin Atil

THE FREER GALLERY OF ART

 Smithsonian Institution, Washington, D.C., 1978

Library of Congress Catalogue No. 78-70427
Copyright © Freer Gallery of Art, 1978

Design/Chaparos Productions Limited
Typesetting/Composition Systems Inc.
Printing/Stephenson, Incorporated
Production/Baker Johnson

Contents

.

Foreword

Artists reveal themselves with disarming candor in their drawings. As faithful records of changes in forms and compositions or as notations of experiments with new imagery, drawings provide insights into an artist's creative processes that cannot be gained in any other way. Neither verbal descriptions nor written records of an artist's work can duplicate the immediacy of the information communicated directly by drawings. In Iran and India, where the names of all but the most famous artists are unknown, drawings are especially important since they offer tantalizing glimpses into those artistic techniques and traditions that were transmitted from generation to generation in imperial studios as well as in provincial workshops.

It is difficult to distinguish Iranian and Indian drawings from paintings, because the artists of those countries used the same materials and techniques for both. In some instances, as with the monochromatic decorative borders of illuminated manuscripts, it becomes all but impossible to make a distinction between the two media.

Since the majority of Iranian and Indian artists were involved in some way with the production of book illustrations, they excelled in the intimate scale of the miniature.

Their drawings constitute the initial statements for paintings that they knew would be studied with the same close attention as the written text. It is not surprising then that the drawings and the finished illustrations were also meant to be "read." Similarly, most of the texts were so familiar to the readers that the heroes, heroines, villains, warriors and deities depicted in the accompanying illustrations were immediately recognizable. For most readers, recognition of the various characters described in the text would be sufficient. Connoisseurs demanded more. Trained to differentiate between the styles of individual artists and schools, Iranian and Indian connoisseurs prided themselves on their ability to detect variations in established traditions or to identify any innovations an artist might introduce. Many innovations or exotic motifs were introduced in the decorative margins of illuminated pages where they would be relatively inconspicuous. Iranian and Indian artists were less inhibited in their drawings, and it is there that they were more apt to explore problems without regard to the strictures of prevailing canons or traditions.

With tradition playing an important role, it was inevitable that Iranian and Indian drawings and paintings should reflect perfection of technique. Yet, technique, in and of itself, was never considered sufficient reason for acclaim. It was an artist's ability to work within the narrow confines of carefully prescribed traditions, not the least of which was the juxtaposition of extraordinary realism and highly conventionalized motifs within the same composition, that occasionally elicited imperial patronage.

Among the Iranian and Indian drawings included in this exhibition are some examples that were acquired by Charles Lang Freer as early as 1907. Mr. Freer's interest in Indian and Iranian drawings at a time when most collectors still paid them scant attention, provides further indication of how enlightened a connoisseur he was. Mr. Freer continued to add to the drawings and paintings in his collection until his death in 1919. Thereafter, the curators of the Gallery were responsible for the growth of the Iranian and Indian collections. Many of the finest drawings included in this exhibition were acquired during the curatorship of Dr. Richard Ettinghausen from 1944 to 1967. Dr. Ettinghausen's discriminating taste and scholarly research were instrumental in raising the Freer Gallery's Iranian and Indian collections to their present position of international eminence. This special exhibition of Iranian and Indian drawings was proposed by Dr. Esin Atıl, the current Curator of Near Eastern Art at the Gallery. She selected the drawings from the collections and prepared the text for the catalogue.

The drawings offer unusual glimpses into many different aspects of life in ancient Iran and India. The subjects range from the dazzling earthly paradises that typified court life, to religious mystics who appear to have been in a state of divine grace. As we study these drawings, we share the artist's reactions to people, to places and to events from a time that is irretrievably past. Because of the intrinsically spontaneous nature of drawings, these people, places and events come alive in a way that is more poignant than in the more hieratic world of miniature paintings.

Thomas Lawton
Director

The Brush of the Masters: Drawings from Iran and India

Drawings from Iran

The earliest drawings made in Iran are found in the marginal decorations of 15th-century imperial manuscripts, as well as on single sheets which were later compiled into albums. The marginal decorations generally employ floral motifs and occasionally animals are placed within the landscape. The only exception to this scheme appears in a unique manuscript, the *Divan* of Sultan Ahmed, the Jalairid ruler whose courts were located in Baghdad and Tabriz. The marginal drawings of the *Divan* contain narrative scenes with figures participating in specific activities and are pictorial representations of the themes expressed in mystic poetry. Executed around 1400, these illustrations depict idyllic settings with nomadic figures, lovers and scholars and include an extraordinary scene with angels bearing celestial fire.

Single-page drawings bound in albums were made during the Turkmen and Timurid periods in diverse centers of the Near East and Central Asia and represent a variety of subjects, including courtly ladies and warriors. Among them is a remarkable group portraying demonic creatures which is associated with the shamanistic traditions of the pre-Islamic peoples of the Asian steppes.

Although these 15th-century drawings were made by anonymous artists, each was executed by a single hand in contrast to contemporary manuscript illustrations, which often reveal the combined efforts of several court painters.

During the Safavid period the artists began to sign their works and the styles of individual painters became identifiable. Sixteenth-century drawings executed in the ateliers of Tabriz and Kazvin depict portraits of solitary figures as well as crowded compositions harmoniously blending a profusion of diverse elements. Studies of single men and women, representing elegant courtly youths in addition to elderly commoners, gradually became more dominant, commissioned by both the members of the court and wealthy citizens.

Patronage has always been an important factor in the development of the arts in the Islamic world, and the shift from imperial sponsorship to that of the middle classes is strikingly noticeable in the 17th century. The artists began to assert their individuality, choose their own subjects and inscribe even the simplest sketch with statements that indicate when and where it was drawn. This highly personal approach characterizes the production of the school of Isfahan, the last Safavid capital, and points to the end of the long tradition of illustrated manuscripts as the individual works of famous artists became sought after by collectors.

Jalairid, Timurid and Turkmen Schools

During the 15th century, Iran was in constant political turmoil with a number of new dynasties rising to power and, shortly after establishing vibrant artistic centers, falling victim to the expansionist policies of the neighboring states. Cities such as Baghdad, Tabriz and Shiraz continually changed hands as the fortunes of a dynasty rose or fell. Yet the 15th century was one of the most brilliant periods in Iranian art; each dynasty produced remarkable sultans who became enthusiastic patrons of the arts, supporting large studios and employing scores of calligraphers and painters.

As the political scene changed and the courts shifted the sites of their capitals, the artists migrated to the new centers and continued to create outstanding works of art. The traditions associated with one school soon merged with those introduced by the emigrés, forming a synthesis which in turn influenced the styles of other schools as the artists moved, or were forced to move, from one court to another.

The confusing political status of the artistic centers also affected the production of their studios. It is often difficult, if not impossible, to identify the provenance of a painting given the heterogeneous nature of the studios and the movement of the artists. Fortunately, there are a few signed and dated examples indicating where they were executed which enable us to more or less define the traditions of a particular school in a particular period.

In order to determine the influences exerted from one tradition to another, it is necessary to present a brief historical account of the major dynasties of the age and to review the status of the artistic centers.

Upon the disintegration of the Ilkhanids, the Mongol rulers of Iran, the Muzaffarids (1314-93) ruled southern Iran from Shiraz until their defeat by the armies of Timur. Another successor state to the Ilkhanids, the Jalairids (1336-1432), controlled western Iran and Irak, establishing courts in Baghdad and Tabriz. Baghdad was particularly creative under the patronage of Sultan Uvays and his son, Ahmed, during the second half of the 14th century. The city was captured twice by Timur who took a number of artists back to his court in Samarkand. The Jalairids were eventually overpowered by the Karakoyunlus, a federation of Turkmen tribes which had originally settled in eastern Anatolia.

The Timurids (1370-1506) ruled supreme in Samarkand, expanding westward from Transoxiana into Iran and Anatolia. Their periodic campaigns not only resulted in territorial gains

but also enriched the Samarkand studios, bringing back a booty of artists. After the death of Timur in 1405, cultural activities shifted to Shiraz and Herat. Herat was chosen as the capital by Shah Rukh, Timur's son, and the governorship of Shiraz was given to Sultan Iskandar, Timur's grandson. Shiraz, which had an active studio during the Muzaffarid period, became a major artistic center when Jalairid artists fled to Iskandar's court following the death of Sultan Ahmed. When Sultan Iskandar was called to Herat in 1414, he took members of his studio with him to the Timurid capital. The Timurid rule in Shiraz lasted until 1453, at which time the city fell to the Karakoyunlus.

Herat flourished under Shah Rukh and his son, Baysunghur. In the painting ateliers there were local artists, as well as those brought from Shiraz by Sultan Iskandar; others arrived in 1420 from Tabriz after a brief Timurid conquest of that city. Herat's greatest period was the last quarter of the 15th century, during the reign of Huseyin Baykara. After his death in 1506, the city was attacked by the Uzbeks and the Safavids who took some of the artists to their respective capitals in Bukhara and Tabriz.

The Karakoyunlu Turkmens (1389-1468) expanded eastward from Anatolia and spread throughout Iran, briefly capturing Herat in 1458. They chose Baghdad as their capital and established a provincial court in Shiraz. The painting studios of Baghdad and Shiraz flourished during the 1450s and 1460s under the patronage of Pir Budak, the son of the last Karakoyunlu sultan, Jahan Shah. In 1467 the Karakoyunlu Turkmens were defeated by another federation of Turkish tribes, the Akkoyunlu Turkmens, who rose to power from Anatolia.

Under the Akkoyunlu rule (1378-1508), Shiraz continued to be an important center until 1478 when the court moved to Tabriz. The Tabriz studios incorporated artists from Shiraz and Herat; Herat had been captured by the Akkoyunlus in 1469. The outstanding patron was Sultan Yakub, and his avid support of the Tabriz studios during the last quarter of the 15th century resulted in the production of a large number of remarkable illustrated manuscripts. The Akkoyunlu empire was terminated in 1501 when Shah Ismail, the founder of the Safavid dynasty, defeated Sultan Ahvand and within a decade brought the whole of Iran under his control.

The most important group of 15th-century drawings from Iran are in the *Divan* of Sultan Ahmed Jalair (nos. 1-7).[1] There is also a series of single leaves, most of which were incorporated into albums (nos. 8-11). These albums include samples of calligraphy, single-page paintings, sketches,

drawings and manuscript illustrations, as well as examples from European and Far Eastern traditions.

Two of the most famous collections, popularly called the "Fatih Albums" since they contain portraits of the Ottoman sultan, Mehmed II ("Fatih" or "the Conqueror"), appear to have been compiled by the Akkoyunlu sultan, Yakub.[2] The paintings in these two albums date from the early years of the 14th to the end of the 15th century. Among them are a group of fascinating tinted drawings bearing the attribution "Mehmed Siyah Kalem," or Mehmed the "Black Pen," that is, one who works with brush and ink.[3] These drawings depict either scenes of nomadic life or fantastic creatures (monsters or demons) engaged in various activities reflecting the shamanistic rites and traditions of Central Asia (no. 10).

The artistic milieu of Baghdad and Tabriz during Sultan Ahmed's reign was extraordinarily creative and innovative. The painters illustrated literary texts, such as the poems of Nizami and Khvaju Kirmani, which did not have earlier established prototypes.[5] The sultan himself was an accomplished musician and poet, writing both in Arabic and Persian. He is said to have carved seals and knew how to paint; he was taught the art of painting by Abd al-Hayy, one of his court painters, and executed a drawing in a manuscript on Abu Said, the last Ilkhanid ruler.

Sultan Ahmed's strong interest in poetry and painting is exemplified in the *Divan,* a collection of his Persian poems. This extraordinary manuscript is the only copy of the work and contains the earliest marginal drawings which are conceived as complete compositions including human figures.

The Divan

When Sultan Ahmed ibn Uvays (1382-1410), the last great ruler of the Jalairid dynasty, ascended the throne, he inherited a highly creative and energetic group of artists, including Shams al-Din, a former student of the celebrated Ahmed Musa. During his relatively long reign, Sultan Ahmed was under constant attack by the Kipchaks, Timurids and Karakoyunlu Turkmens.[4] The sultan was able to survive these defeats by escaping to the Ottoman or Mamluk courts and avoiding direct confrontation. He was killed in 1410 while fighting against Kara Yusuf of the Karakoyunlus in a final attempt to save his domain. Soon after his death, the Jalairid lands were divided between the Karakoyunlus and the Timurids.

In spite of the political turmoil of his reign, Sultan Ahmed managed to sponsor a series of outstanding illustrated

1-7. The *Divan* of Sultan Ahmed Jalair
Iran, Jalairid period, ca. 1400

Page: 29.2 x 20.3 cm.
  (11½ x 8 in.)
Text: 18.5 x 11.5 cm.
  (7¼ x 4½ in.)
337 folios, contemporary binding, illuminated heading (32.29); eight folios with marginal drawings (32.30-32.37)

manuscripts and to support renowned artists. Among them were Junayd and Abd al-Hayy, the painters who had been trained by Shams al-Din, and the calligrapher Mir Ali of Tabriz, who is credited with the invention of the *nastalik* script. The artists of Sultan Ahmed's court were so highly regarded that Timur took a group of them to Samarkand when he conquered Baghdad. Following the death of Sultan Ahmed, a number of painters joined the court of Sultan Iskandar, the Timurid governor of Shiraz. Several masters appear to have remained in Baghdad and Tabriz, seeking employment under the new rulers, the Karakoyunlus. The stylistic features determined by the Jalairid artists of the court of Sultan Ahmed were influential in the development of Timurid and Turkmen schools of painting.

The manuscript contains 337 folios written in a fine *nastalik* script; eight of the folios have marginal drawings rendered in black ink with slight touches of blue and gold (fols. 17a, 18a, 19a, 21b, 22b, 23a, 24a and 25b).[6] The work was rebound at a later date but the original cover was retained during the restoration. Presently, the binding has a modern spine and lacks the traditional flap attached to the back cover. The bookbinding is a brown leather on pasteboard with stamped and tooled decoration and contains traces of gilding. The central ogival medallion and corner quadrants decorating the exterior of the front cover are filled with arabesques, enclosed by several braided and interlacing bands. Although the layout of the exterior of the back cover is identical, the central medallion depicts a landscape with a deer and doe; a crouching hare appears amidst foliage in each of the corner quadrants. The enclosing bands are also varied, using floral scrolls as well as braiding. The interiors of both covers are enhanced with reddish-brown leather; filigree work, embellished with gold cartouches and placed over a blue ground, decorates the central medallion and corner quadrants.

The work begins with an illuminated heading (fol. 1b) and contains the poems of Sultan Ahmed who practiced different forms, such as the *mathnavi* (couplet), *kasida* (monorhythmic poem), *ghazal* (ode), *rubai* (quatrain) and *kita* (fragment). Gold and blue lines are used around the text leaving wide margins; there is an additional border of blue and red lines, and on the folios with marginal illustrations, they are drawn over the scenes. Gold lines separate the poems and divide the hemistichs. The poet's name is also rendered in gold and appears as "Ahmed," "Ahmed Uvays" or "Ibn Uvays"; in the *ghazals,* the name is always in the last line in accordance with Iranian practice.

Each poem begins with the following phrase: "and by him too, may God Almighty make his caliphate and sultanate abide forever," executed in gold, blue or red; occasionally only the word "caliphate" is used, or the order is reversed to read "sultanate and caliphate."

The works of Sadi have been added to the wide margins of the text, beginning on folio 2a and ending on folio 311a where the date of this later addition is given as 1643. The red and blue lines around the margins also belong to this date and terminate on folio 311a. The remaining 26 folios have blank margins. There are also several blank, or almost blank, folios toward the end of the manuscript.

The text lacks a colophon, but on the last page (fol. 337b) there are two notations, executed by different hands, which give information on the date of the manuscript and its copyist. The notation on the very top of the folio states: "the book was finished with the help of God, the Giver, in the month of Ramazan, in the year eight and five hundred in Hijra of the Prophet, God bless him." The date "eight and five hundred," or 508 Hijra, corresponds to 1114 A.D.; however, if it was intended to be 805 Hijra, then the year 1402 A.D. is given, which falls within the reign of Sultan Ahmed. The month of Ramazan, 805 Hijra, corresponds to March-April, 1402 A.D.

The second notation, written on an angle on the lower portion of the folio, reads: "the handwriting of Mir Ali, mercy be upon him." It refers to the famous Mir Ali of Tabriz who worked in the court of Sultan Ahmed and copied the poems of Khvaju Kirmani for the sultan.[7] Since this work and the Freer *Divan* reveal the same style of writing, there is no reason to doubt the validity of the attribution.

The flyleaf at the beginning of the manuscript and the last folio of the text possess several seals. Only the one on the last folio is clear enough to decipher: it is an Ottoman *tuğra* (royal seal), identified as that of Sultan Beyazid II (1481-1512), which indicates that this volume once belonged to the imperial collections of the Topkapi Palace in Istanbul.

Very little is known about the history of the work prior to the 20th century; in 1912 it was purchased in Istanbul by F. R. Martin, and in 1932 it entered the collection of the Freer Gallery of Art. The reconstruction of the early history of the *Divan* is purely conjectural: it may have passed into the hands of the Karakoyunlu Turkmens after they defeated and killed Sultan Ahmed, then to the Akkoyunlus who put an end to the Karakoyunlus in 1467. Since the work contains the *tuğra* of Sultan Beyazid II, it could have been presented to him by

the last Akkoyunlu sultan, Ahvand, who fled to the Ottoman court after his defeat by Shah Ismail in 1501. The *Divan* remained in the Ottoman Palace, or at least in Istanbul, until it was obtained by Martin in the early years of the 20th century.

The eight marginal drawings, executed in fine brushwork, are conceived as complete scenes filling the entire surface of the folios. Although positioned around the text, the scenes appear as if the poems are placed over them, harmoniously extending under and around the text. Similar to the other examples of manuscript illustration executed in the court of Sultan Ahmed, the drawings reveal a new concept in painting: small figures are placed within a landscape setting which extends high into the horizon; a multitude of elements are integrated into the scenes, creating rich but spacious compositions. These features, determined by the Jalairid painters, were fully developed in the Turkmen and Timurid courts.

The lyric quality of the drawings parallels the themes of the poems which are mystical in nature, exhalting love and praising the Creator. The drawings are not "illustrations" of the text but pictorial representations of the sentiments expressed by the poet. In a recent publication by Deborah Klimburg-Salter, they have been interpreted as depicting scenes from the *Mantik al-Tayr* (Conversation of Birds) by Attar in which 30 birds (symbols of mankind) undertake a spiritual journey in search of God, passing through seven stages or valleys. In this study, the artist has been identified as Abd al-Hayy who worked in the studio of Sultan Ahmed in Baghdad and was a master in the art of drawing.[8]

The placement of the drawings within the manuscript is rather curious; they are clustered together between folios 17 and 25. It is possible that the entire *Divan* was meant to be adorned with marginal drawings since the folios have exceptionaliy wide margins. The artist may have executed a small portion, almost one signature, before the manuscript was collated and bound.

There is also no logical explanation for the six empty folios toward the end of the book.[9] The suggestion that they were left blank for illustrations seems unlikely; the placement of the paintings in these locations would have been most untraditional for Islamic manuscripts. Perhaps additional poems were to be included and the author was still engaged in refining them while the calligrapher copied the finished ones. The work on the manuscript must have been interrupted by the political disorders of the age, most likely by the 1401 sack of Baghdad by Timur.

1. Pastoral Scene

Black line on paper
32.30 (fol. 17a)

The drawing depicts a country scene with a flock of geese flying over the landscape. On the left, an old man leaning on a staff accompanies a woman carrying a child. Below them are a pair of water buffaloes and a body of water with several ducks. On the lower right, two more buffaloes approach the water; a young man, riding one of the animals, holds their reins and guides them with a stick.

The scene is executed in fine brushwork with varied intensity of pigment. Certain elements—such as the outlines of the hills, clusters of bushes and blades of grass—are defined in darker strokes while washes and softer tones are used in modeling the landscape and figures. A feeling of depth is created by the suggestion of receding planes, moving from the water in the foreground to the hills placed high on the horizon.

The vignette of a young man guiding buffaloes resembles the theme employed in Far Eastern painting. Cultural exchanges between Iran and Central Asia had been established during the Il-khanid period, and a number of Far Eastern features are frequently encountered in 14th- and 15th-century paintings.

The scene has been interpreted by Deborah Klimburg-Salter as representing the Valley of the Quest from Attar's *Mantik al-Tayr*. It symbolizes the first stage in the spiritual journey in search of God.

در لطف تو كس سخن نذارد   كرمت سخن در ان د

2. Landscape with Two Couples

Black line on paper
32.31 (fol. 18a)

A plane tree in full bloom with birds fluttering about its branches extends around and under the text. On the left, a youth leaning against a barren tree converses with a young woman. Below them is a tray with two bottles of wine, an incense burner and a bowl of fruit next to an empty bed covered with carpets and cushions. On the lower right, another woman reclines against a cushion while a second man, lost in thought, sits behind the trunk of a tree.

Similar to the previous example, this scene is executed in varying tones of black pigment with no additional color. The empty and disorderly bed, together with fruit and wine, suggest that it was recently used by the couples. The theme is identified as the symbolic representation of the Valley of Love, the second state in Attar's mystical poem.

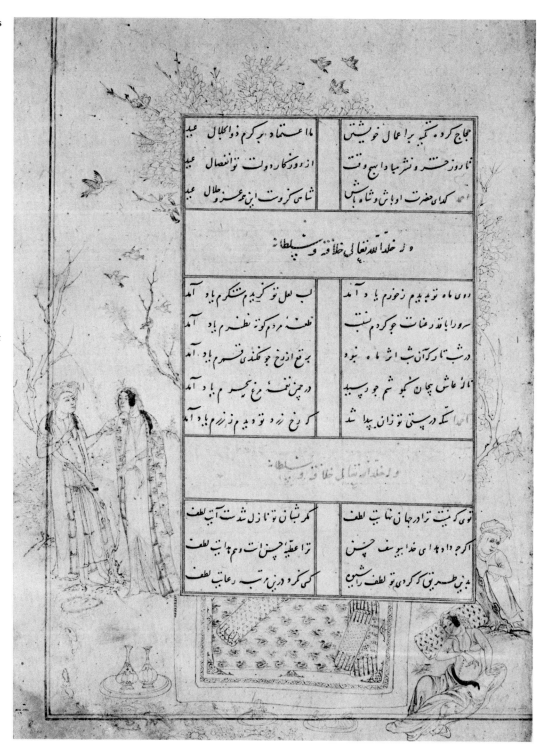

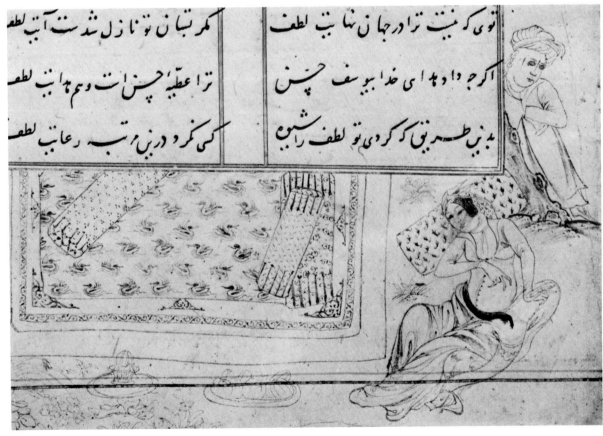

تویی کز نیت ترا در جهان نهایت لطف
کمر تبان تو نازل شدست آتب لطف

اگر جز داده‌ای خدا بیوسف چشن
ترا عطیه چشنات وهم جانب لطف

بدین طریقی که کردی تو لطف را شبین
کسی کرد درین مرتبه رعایتب لطف

3. Gathering of Scholars

Black line on paper
32.32 (fol. 19a)

Similar to the previous drawing, a fully foliated plane tree teeming with birds grows around and under the text. On the lower left, a pair of bearded figures hold a discussion while seated on a carpet with several books piled in front. Below them, three men listen to a couple of personages who hold additional books. On the lower right, next to the tree trunk, is a terrace with a carved balustrade and a bunch of flowers growing from its upper edge.

Scholars and sages holding discussions under a plane tree are commonly seen in the illustrations of contemporary literary texts. This scene is thought to depict the Valley of Understanding in which knowledge is sought.

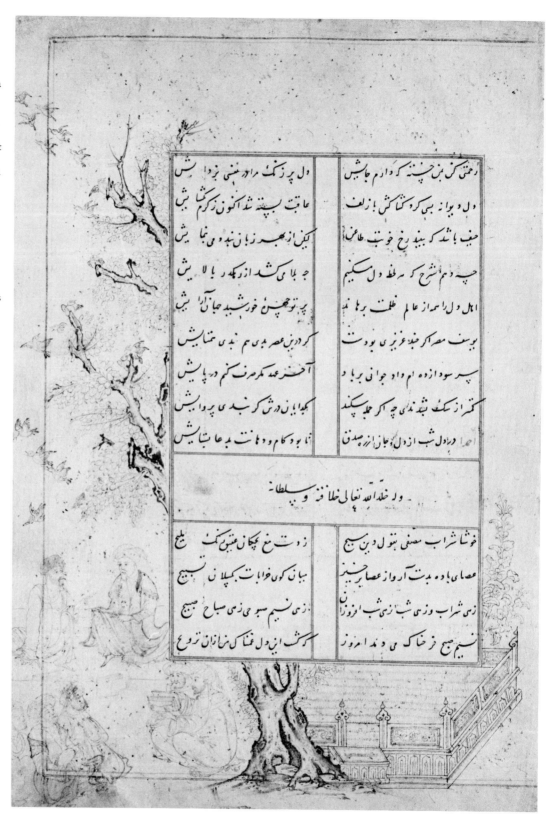

4. Angels Amidst Clouds

Black line and gold on paper;
tinted with red and blue
32.33 (fol. 21b)

A stream of golden clouds flows
down the right margin of the
folio, filling the lower portion.
Three angels peer from the opening of the sky on the top while 12
others ride down with the clouds.
Two figures on the lower portion
carry flaming torches or incense
burners.

The sky, wings of the angels and
some of their garments are rendered in blue; a brownish red is
used on several other garments.
The extensive use of gold in the
clouds, bursting through the
folio, is quite remarkable and possibly represents the Divine Light.

The theme represented here is the
Valley of Astonishment in which
neither man nor beast dwells.
This valley is the sixth stage in
Attar's work and appears out of
sequence in the *Divan*. Six lines of
text in the upper left margin and
the catchwords below belong to
the 17th-century addition of the
works of Sadi.

5.-6. Camp Scene

Black line on paper; tinted with
   red and blue
32.34-32.35 (fols. 22b-23a)

This pair of drawings, representing the activities of a nomad
camp, is the only scene in the
Divan which spreads to double
folios. The right portion depicts
the actual camp whereas the left
describes the surroundings. On
the upper right are four tents with
their convertible hoods partially
or completely open for ventila-
tion; smoke from one of the tents
escapes through the opening.
Strolling around the structures are
a pair of women and a bearded
man guiding his cow. Below him,
an elderly woman tends the herd.

On the lower right, a couple is
busy setting up their tent, attach-
ing the convertible hood and
tightening the girdle around the
structure. Seated next to them is a
young mother holding her infant
while a pair of children play in
front. On the lower left, a woman
blows the fire lit under a large
kettle whereas her companion
washes clothes at the edge of a
river; behind them are several
dogs tied by a leash.

On the lower portion of the facing
folio, a pair of figures bring more
firewood. The margin on the far
left depicts the animals of the
nomads: long-haired sheep or
goats with large horns run about
while several horses graze or rest.
A horseman on the upper left
holds a long whip and waves at
his friends; next to him, a woman
converses with another man who
is riding a cow. The margins between the two folios are handled
as a unit: on the right an elderly
man holding a stick and a woman
carrying a bowl walk toward the
man who stands on the facing
page, next to his flock.

24

Touches of blue appear in the grass growing on the banks of the river in the foreground and clustered around the tree as well as in the clouds, plants and foliage filling the left page. The fine red lines seen on the garment and headdress of the horseman holding the whip and on one of the tents seem to be later additions.

These folios depict the setting of a nomad camp, its activities and inhabitants in great detail and accuracy. The artist has clearly represented the construction of the tents and their decoration; the men, women and children of the tribe and their function within the system; the domesticated sheep, goats and cattle, plus the horses and dogs which are essential to the existence of the group. Although a multitude of elements and vignettes fill the margins, the scene is not overcrowded. It represents the utopian harmony of man and nature as expressed in Attar's Valley of Detachment, the fourth stage in the journey of the birds.

وله

تا سواد زلف عنبر فام ز

قد سروش دیب اند و سرورا

ثنا می چین و ملاحت را بد

7. River Scene

Black line on paper
32.37 (fol. 25b)

This scene is devoid of human representation and depicts a landscape with birds flying over a winding river in which a pair of ducks swim. On the upper portion, cranes and geese fly through swirling clouds, while on the right, several other species of birds and butterflies hover around the trees and shrubs growing at the edge of the river. The river swings down the margin and flows into the lower portion. A tree and pair of birds appear on the left margin.

The harmonious juxtaposition of the elements suggests the fifth stage in Attar's work which describes the Valley of Unity where all forces of nature follow a single rhythm.

The remaining illustration from the *Divan* (32.36, fol. 24a) originally depicted a river scene with several ducks, and could have represented the seventh and last stage in the *Mantik al-Tayr,* the Valley of Nothingness, beyond which one can go no further. The margins of this folio are now completely covered with the works of Sadi which almost camouflage the delicate drawing. Two female figures were added to the small squares on either side of the last couplet in the text.

8. Warrior

Iran or Central Asia, Turkmen or
   Timurid period, 15th century

Black line and gold on paper;
   tinted with red and pink
Page: 38.7 x 23 cm.
   (15¼ x 9⅟₁₆ in.)
Drawing: 24.3 x 13.5 cm.
   (9⁹⁄₁₆ x 5⁵⁄₁₆ in.)
29.79

This drawing, removed from an
album, is enclosed by several
borders and pasted on a deep-blue
sheet decorated with gold floral
motifs. The page has been backed
with a blank piece of cardboard.

The figure represents a Mongol or
Tatar warrior, attired in a helmet,
belted tunic, short pants and
low-heeled shoes. He is fully
equipped with the weapons of his
profession: he holds a shield and
sword and carries a bow around
his neck while a hatchet hangs
over his arm; tucked into his belt
are a dagger and the scabbard of
the sword. The figure appears to
be running to the left, one foot
firmly planted on the ground
whereas the other is lifted.

The face, hands and bare legs are
tinted pink; red dots decorate his
helmet and the scabbard; gold is
used in the metal parts of his
weapons and garments, as well as
on his helmet, collar, sash and
shoes. He wears a large earring
and gold beads adorn his headdress.

There exists an identical drawing
executed in the Ottoman court
during the 17th century.[10] The
Turkish figure is the same size,
indicating that it was traced or
copied from the Freer drawing,
which must have been formerly a
part of the Istanbul albums.

9. Women with Tea Service

Iran or Central Asia, Turkmen or
  Timurid period, 15th century

Black line and gold on paper;
  tinted with red, blue and green
Page: 40.4 x 28 cm.
  15⅞ x 11 in.)
Drawing: 19.6 x 15.9 cm.
  (7¾ x 6¼ in.)
38.14

The drawing, enclosed by several
borders, is pasted on an album
leaf which has wide margins decorated with gold floral designs on a
beige ground. Two samples of
calligraphy appear on the back.

The woman on the left carries a
tray with several covered bowls
while her companion holds a
strange-looking teapot. Both
woman have elaborate headdresses; pearls, ribbons, streamers
and tassels adorn their hair. They
are dressed in loosely belted
jackets and long skirts, wear hob-
nailed shoes and bear archer's
rings on their thumbs. Their
facial features suggest that they
are of Central Asian or Far Eastern
origin.

The representation of their garments with highly decorative
folds and drapery, peculiar
hairstyles and confusing tea
equipage indicate that the drawing was executed by an artist re-
motely familiar with Asian
women and depicted what he
thought they looked like.

Gold is used exclusively on the
teapot, on the lids of the tea
bowls and in the long dangling
earrings (?) of the lady on the
right. Touches of pale red, blue
and green appear on the garments, hair ornaments and tray.

This drawing may have been executed in Samarkand during the
Timurid period or in Tabriz under
the patronage of the Akkoyunlu
Turkmens. A number of similar
examples appear in the Istanbul
albums where this piece might
have originated.

10. Two Fettered Demons

Iran or Central Asia, Turkmen or
  Timurid period, 15th century

Black line and gold on paper;
  tinted with red and blue
14.6 x 22.1 cm. (5¾ x 8¹¹⁄₁₆ in.)
37.25

The drawing, cut to the edge and
mounted on a larger sheet of
blank paper, is typical of the
series in the Istanbul albums
which bear the attribution
"Mehmed Siyah Kalem" although
revealing variations in style and
subject matter. A group of these
drawings represents fantastic
beings (monsters or demons) who
are shown singing, dancing or
playing musical instruments. The
Freer example is unusual in that
the demons are shown in shackles
while enjoying the pleasures of
wine and music.[11]

There is a pathetic quality in the
representation of the creatures;
even though bound in chains,
they are attempting to amuse
themselves, accepting their fate as
prisoners.

The half-naked figures are seated
on the ground. One of them holds
a blue-and-white porcelain bottle
and offers a drink in a fluted cup
to his companion; the other plays
a type of string instrument which
is frequently depicted in the
series. Below them are two animal
legs with hoofs, used in making
music by the shamans of Central
Asia.

The bodies of the figures are executed in fine brushwork and
washes. The demon on the right
has a skirt drawn in blue whereas
his partner's garment is in pale
brownish red. Thickly applied

gold paint with tooled decoration
appears in the armlets, bracelets
and shackles of the demons as well
as in the string instrument, wine
cup and handles of the animal
legs.

The design on the porcelain bottle, depicting a freely drawn
dragon, can be traced to the Yüan
dynasty (1280-1386), when the
Mongols ruled China, and was
popular in the ensuing Ming
period. Blue-and-white Chinese
wares were very much in demand
throughout the Near East and
were imported in large quantities
and collected by the rulers. The
Istanbul albums contain a number
of paintings in which similar
blue-and-white Chinese porcelains
are depicted.

لتصوير محمدت . پادشاه

11. Galloping Horseman
Iran, Turkmen or Timurid period,
  late 15th century

Black line and gold on paper;
  tinted with red
10.1 x 15.4 cm. (4 x 6¹/₁₆ in.)
47.22

This extremely fine drawing represents a rider urging his mount with a short whip commonly used by Turkmen or Mongol horsemen. The illustration is trimmed to the edge and mounted on cardboard.

Inscribed on both sides is a later attribution which reads: "portrait of Muhammed (or Mehmed) Shah, Padishah." Muhammed was a popular name among the 15th-century rulers, used by the Turkmens and the Jalairids as well as by the Khans of the Golden Horde who ruled south Russia. The word *padishah*, or the great

shah, was employed from the 15th century onward by the Ottomans. Since the drawing resembles several other examples included in the Istanbul albums, this inscription was likely added in the Ottoman court and could refer to a number of Muhammeds or Mehmeds, including the Ottoman sultans.

The figure is attired in garments of the period: he wears a cap with its split-rim turned down, a short-sleeved jacket over a long-sleeved shirt, pants and boots. A bow and quiver with arrows hang at his side while a long staff is tucked into his belt.

Black lines define most of the elements; pale red is used to outline the horse trappings, saddle and saddlecloth as well as the quiver, boots and whip of the rider. Bright red strokes accen-

tuate the tiny feathers on the arrows tucked into the quiver.

The horse is depicted in full gallop, running breathlessly with its mouth open. The hoofs on its inner legs are turned upward revealing the horseshoes and nails. Although the theme of a galloping horseman is common in 15th-century paintings, the turned-up hoofs are unusual. This particular view appears on several "Mehmed Siyah Kalem" drawings which represent contorted horses with twisted legs.

Safavid Period

The Safavid dynasty (1501-1732) rose from a sufi, or mystic, origin established in the middle of the 14th century by Sheykh Safi al-Din. It became a major power during the reign of Ismail (1501-24), who succeeded in bringing the whole of Iran under his rule despite the threats by the Ottomans in the west and the Uzbeks in the northeast. Shah Ismail conquered Tabriz in 1502, made it his capital and occupied Shiraz the following year. In 1510 he entered Herat and sent a substantial group of Timurid artists back to his capital. Tabriz, which was an important artistic center during the Akkoyunlu rule, flourished under the patronage of Ismail's son and heir, Shah Tahmasp (1524-76).

The early works of the Safavid capital relied on the Akkoyunlu style of Tabriz. Shah Ismail himself was brought up within that artistic environment, having married into the Akkoyunlu family. After the arrival of artists from Herat, a new and vibrant school of painting developed, blending the best of both traditions. Shah Tahmasp had been educated in Herat and brought to the capital his enthusiasm for the arts. He was particularly interested in illustrated manuscripts and supported the painting activities of the court. The artists of his studio executed the illustrations in a monumental volume of Firdausi's *Shahname* and worked on a number of other literary texts, including the collection of poems written by such celebrated authors as Hafiz and Nizami.[12]

Herat, occupied several times by the Uzbeks, remained in Safavid hands, and artists there continued to create exquisite works rivaling those of Tabriz.[13] Shiraz was also extremely active, producing at first works in the style of the Akkoyunlu school, then following the Safavid tradition established in Tabriz. Single paintings and drawings became quite popular, and many were collected in albums compiled by Shah Tahmasp and his brother, Bahram Mirza.[14]

Tabriz was on the Safavid border and exposed to recurring Ottoman attacks. In 1514 Sultan Selim captured the city and took a large group of artists to his court in Istanbul. The ensuing sultan, Süleyman the Magnificent, entered the city several times (in 1534, 1538 and 1548), forcing Shah Tahmasp to move the Safavid court to the safety of Kazvin after the last Ottoman attack.

The school of Kazvin initially continued the tradition practiced in Tabriz. However, it soon developed a characteristic manner of representation, depicting elaborate landscapes with thin, tall and elegant figures. During the second half of the 16th century, the studios of Herat and Meshhed were also creative, producing outstanding manuscripts. The artists of Herat were supported by Shah Tahmasp's brother, Sam Mirza, and those in Meshhed were under the patronage of the shah's nephew and son-in-law, Ibrahim Mirza. It was Ibrahim Mirza who commissioned one of the last great illustrated manuscripts, a magnificent copy of Jami's *Haft Avrang* owned by the Freer Gallery of Art.[15]

Following the death of Shah Tahmasp, internal and external disturbances weakened the Safavid rule during the reigns of Ismail II (1576-78) and Muhammed Khudabanda (1578-87). The empire was consolidated and its power reinstated by Shah Abbas (1587-1629) who moved the court in 1598 to Isfahan, which under his patronage became a brilliant cultural center.[16]

Shah Abbas, like his grandfather, Tahmasp, was brought up in Herat, which retained its artistic traditions and activities even though the capitals of the Safavids were always in western Iran. The shah's early education in Herat most likely contributed to his interest in the arts. Isfahan was embellished with spectacular jewel-like buildings and gardens, and its painting studios enjoyed a large and varied clientele, supported by the court, members of the aristocracy, wealthy citizens and foreign collectors. The production of illustrated manuscripts was secondary to single paintings and drawings which were becoming increasingly popular. Drawings were by far the greatest in demand, depicting idyllic scenes as well as mundane subjects. The works were frequently inscribed with the date and the name of the artist and often contained lengthy statements describing the environment in which they were executed.

After the death of Shah Abbas, the Safavid Empire began a slow but steady decline. Abbas had a morbid fear of being overthrown by his heirs and eliminated all his sons. His grandson and successor, Safi I (1629-42), was brought up in the harem due to the shah's paranoia and was virtually unfit to rule. Yet the workshops established by Abbas remained active regardless of the lack of stimulating and demanding patronage. The artists continued producing illustrated manuscripts and single paintings which toward the end of the 17th century began to follow the new Europeanizing trends.

The Safavid rule came to an end when the governor of Afghanistan declared his independence, and his son, Mahmud, invaded Isfahan in 1722. Various members of the Safavid house were left as puppet rulers for another decade, but the effective rule of the dynasty ended with the fall of Isfahan.

Iran was on the verge of collapse when a remarkable man rose to the occasion and reestablished its territorial integrity. Nadir Shah, formerly in the service of the Safavids, cleared the land of foreign invaders and established his own dynasty, the Afsharids (1736-95). After Nadir Shah's death in 1747, his heirs were able to rule only in eastern Iran, and the country became divided between various military chiefs. The Zands (1750-94) held the southern regions until the rise of a

Turkmen tribe, the Kajars (1779-1924), who succeeded in controlling the whole of Iran.

The earliest drawings executed during the Safavid period were made in Tabriz, most likely for the imperial albums favored by Shah Tahmasp and his brother, Bahram Mirza (no. 12). The studios of the second capital, Kazvin, and those of the provincial courts in Herat and Meshhed also produced drawings which were fashionable during the second half of the 16th century (nos. 13-16). A number of examples bear the signatures of the artists, including Muhammedi and Sheykh Muhammed, both of whom executed single-page paintings and tinted drawings (nos. 15, 15A, 16, 16A).

Muhammedi is said to have been the pupil as well as the son of the greatest painter of the age, Sultan Muhammed of Tabriz, who worked in the court of Shah Tahmasp. An inscription on a copy of one of Muhammedi's paintings made by Riza mentions that the artist was from Herat, but little else is known about his life and activities.[17] According to his dated paintings, he was active between 1527 and 1584.[18] His early style is very close to that of Sultan Muhammed and as a young man he must have made several paintings and drawings while still living in Herat. One of these early works is a portrait of a youth in the Freer Gallery of Art and another is a drawing of an angel in Boston.[19] He is also mentioned as having painted lacquer bookbindings which were coming into fashion in the Safavid court.

Muhammedi was a master of single-page paintings and drawings, and there are a number of examples either attributed to him or bearing his signature. An album leaf in Boston contains a figure of a man holding a drawing and a pen with an inscription that states: "the work of Muhammedi, the portrait of Muhammedi."[20] His signed paintings depict lovers in a landscape or individual portraits of men or women, including a young prince in a brocaded coat in the collection of the Freer Gallery of Art (no. 15A).[21] Among his signed drawings are studies of mystics and dervishes and an outstanding representation of a pastoral scene which bears the date 1578.[22] Muhammedi reached his mature style around 1575, during the reign of Tahmasp's brother, Shah Ismail II.

Sheykh Muhammed was the son of a calligrapher and studied painting with the famous Dust Muhammed, one of Shah Tahmasp's court artists. He worked in Tabriz and Kazvin under several royal patrons until the turn of the century. His earliest paintings are thought to be in Shah Tahmasp's *Shahname* executed during the 1530s and 1540s. Sheykh Muhammed's fully developed style is seen in Ibrahim Mirza's *Haft Avrang* which was copied in Meshhed, Kazvin and Herat between 1556 and 1565. In the last quarter of the 16th century, the artist joined the ateliers of Shah Ismail II and

Shah Abbas. Sheykh Muhammed's only signed and dated painting, executed in 1556-57, is in the Freer Gallery of Art (no. 16A).

The artist is said to have imitated Chinese styles and was the first to introduce European painting traditions into Iran; however, we have no evidence of these activities. His signature appears on three drawings, one of which, representing a kneeling youth holding a parakeet, is included in the exhibition (no. 16). The second example is almost identical, depicting a youth with a book, while the third represents a dervish.[23] Sheykh Muhammed's paintings also influenced Riza who copied one of his drawings.[24]

Drawings from the school of Isfahan are far more numerous and include many signed and dated examples, such as those made by Mirza Muhammed al-Huseyni (no. 18), Muhammed Muhsin (nos. 25 and 26), Riza (nos. 19, 28-33) and Muin Musavvir (nos. 26 and 34).

Muhammed Muhsin appears to have been working in Isfahan in the middle of the 17th century since two of his signed drawings bear the date 1649 (no. 24).[25] A reference to this artist mentions that he was from Tabriz and studied with the calligrapher Mahmud Shahabi who died in 1583 in Herat, his native town.[26] Another source states that Muhammed Muhsin "al-Arshi" was a calligrapher who worked in Isfahan and died in 1680.[27] If these two men are one and the same, then the artist first studied in Herat and later moved to Isfahan. He also had an exceptionally long life. An album page in the India Office Library contains a sheet of calligraphy signed by Muhammed Muhsin "al-Haravi," that is, from Herat.[28] Two drawings of dervishes are attributed to him, one of which bears the name Muhsin.[29] The artist appears to have been a calligrapher as well as a painter, which was not unusual in the Safavid period.

The most prolific and influential painter of the Isfahan court school was Riza, who signed his name either as Aka Riza or as Riza-i Abbasi; according to his dated works, the artist was active between 1587 and 1639.[30] He was born around 1565 in Meshhed; his father, Ali Asghar, was a painter in the ateliers of Ibrahim Mirza and Shah Ismail II. Riza appears to have joined the court of Shah Abbas in 1587 and immediately set to work on a royal *Shahname* (ca. 1587-97).[31] Although his paintings appear in other illustrated manuscripts—such as the *Kisas al-Anbiya* (ca. 1600), the *Divan* of Ali Shir Nevai (ca. 1620) and the *Khosrau va Shirin* (dated 1632)[32]—he is far better known for his single-page studies. These paintings are characteristic of the style of the school of Isfahan, generally representing single figures lost in their own dreamworlds (nos. 19A and 19B). His drawings, executed in delicate and sinuous lines, depict figures in rather exaggerated poses (nos. 19, 27-33).

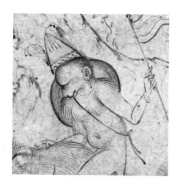

Riza abandoned his career in the royal atelier around 1605, taking up with lowbred companions in preference to the affected elite of the court. He returned to his profession in 1615 and produced an enormous number of single-page drawings until his death, which occurred about 1640. His works were copied and imitated by such a large group of followers that the school of Isfahan became identified with that of Riza.

Muin Musavvir was the most gifted of Riza's numerous students and followers and possibly the last great Safavid painter. His dated works fall between 1635 and 1707, and during his long career he worked in the traditional manner, avoiding the Europeanizing trend which was popular among his contemporaries. Muin was a great draftsman and an excellent painter, executing single-page drawings and paintings as well as manuscript illustrations, including several copies of the *Shahname* and a history of Shah Ismail.[33] His drawings are far more numerous than his paintings and generally depict studies of single figures (nos. 26 and 34).

The majority of the drawings from the late Safavid period owned by the Freer Gallery of Art belong to a collection popularly called the "Riza-i Abbasi Album." The album consists of 60 drawings mounted on 49 sheets, seven of which have two to four small sketches pasted together (53.12-53.60).

The work was formerly in the collection of Friedrich Sarre who published a monograph in 1914 which included an extensive study on the album and facsimiles of the drawings.[34] The author states that the drawings were bound in a lacquer binding dating from the first half of the 18th century and suggests that the album was compiled at that time. Irregular strips of red and buff paper were used to frame the drawings, which were pasted on coarse cardboard leaves measuring 26.4 by 18.6 centimeters (10⅜ by 7⁵⁄₁₆ inches); these leaves were attached to one another in a concertina-form, a most unusual format for Near Eastern manuscripts. However, on one of the drawings there is a later inscription which gives the name of the owner and the date 1297 Hijra, that is, 1879 A.D. (no. 28). Therefore, the album was assembled in the last quarter of the 19th century which accounts for its unconventional manner of compilation. The drawings must have been pasted on cardboard sheets cut to fit the 18th-century lacquer bookbinding. When the album was purchased by the Freer Gallery of Art in 1953, it was already unbound and the leaves separated; the binding and four of the drawings illustrated in Sarre's book were also missing.[35]

The collection contains a number of signed and dated drawings and sketches, ranging from 1598 to 1643. Among the dated examples are several bearing the names of Riza and Muin, while the remaining appear to belong to Riza's school

and show a close affinity to the master's style. The majority of the drawings were made during the reign of Safi I, the successor and grandson of Shah Abbas.

Included in the exhibition are 34 sheets, four of which have a pair of drawings pasted together (nos. 27-60; double drawings nos. 37, 39, 47 and 54). The drawings in the exhibition are arranged in groups of signed and dated examples (nos. 27-34), dated pieces (nos. 35-44), those that have written comments (nos. 45-47) and others without any inscriptions (nos. 48-60). Seven of them bear inscriptions giving the name of the artist as Riza, Riza-i Abbasi or Aka Riza (nos. 27-33). With one exception (no. 32), these drawings are dated between 1598 and 1639, covering a major portion of the painter's life. Three other examples contain the name of Muina, identified as Muin Musavvir, and are dated 1639-43. One of them was made by Muin himself (no. 34), whereas the inscriptions on the other two indicate that they were either executed in his house or contain a reference to him (nos. 37 and 44).

Since the drawings in the album cover a period of at least 55 years, there is quite a variation in the tone of the papers, subject matter, manner of execution and style of writing. The papers, uniformly polished, range from pale cream and buff to a deeper tone which is almost tan; one scene is painted on a colored sheet (no. 46). Some of the drawings are obviously finished examples and contain the names of the persons who commissioned them. They were generally ordered by unknown personages, such as wealthy merchants and doctors (nos. 27, 29 and 35); only one example states that it was specifically made for the Imperial Treasury (no. 33). Several are sketches for manuscript illustrations, such as the *Layla va Majnun* and *Yusuf va Zulaykha* series (nos. 38 and 60), or book decorations (nos. 57 and 58). A number of examples have fine pierced holes following the lines, indicating that they were used as stencils (nos. 29, 56 and 58). White lead was employed for correction on several drawings and appears now as a dark-gray stain on the paper (no. 47).

Black line is used on a majority of the examples although there are a few rendered in red and black or solely in red; rarely do the scenes reveal polychrome tints. The style of inscriptions vary; some are almost as sketchy as the drawings and quite difficult to read. It is surprising that the inscriptions are so highly detailed and precise, giving the exact day the drawings were made, in whose house and under what conditions. This extraordinarily informative manner of inscribing the drawings is a characteristic feature of the period.

Although the inscription of one example states that it was made in Meshhed (no. 27) and another in Herat (no. 45), the entire album follows the style identified with the school of Isfahan.

12. Ascension of Solomon
Iran, Safavid period, early 16th century

Black line and gold on paper; tinted with red, blue and green
Page: 35 x 24 cm.
(13¾ x 9⁷⁄₁₆ in.)
Drawing: 30.8 x 19.8 cm.
(12⅛ x 7¹³⁄₁₆ in.)
50.1

The drawing, mounted on heavy paper and framed with several gold lines, represents the celestial journey of a crowned figure seated on an octagonal throne. Accompanying him are various winged creatures: *peris* (fairies or angels) and *jinns* (genies or demons), who either play musical instruments, bear vessels with offerings or carry animals. The composition is almost concentric with the elements radiating from and swirling around the central personage.

A strip of land appears on the lower edge of the scene with jagged hills and vegetation among which a rabbit sleeps peacefully. Immediately above are winged figures carrying diverse animals and birds such as deer, leopard, mountain goat, peacock and duck; one of the figures bears a long-necked bottle on a tray. In the second register are three *peris* who hold covered bowls and a plate of fruit; behind them is a dancer with a pair of clappers who sways to the music of a trio which includes horn, lute and tambourine players.

The crowned figure is in the center of the scene, his throne carried by a pair of *peris*. Two figures hold a billowing canopy over his head; surrounding the throne are other attendants who play a flute, carry a fan or incense burner, or lead the way. A horned creature flies in front of the group which is followed by a four-armed *peri* holding a lute, wine bottle, and cup and saucer.

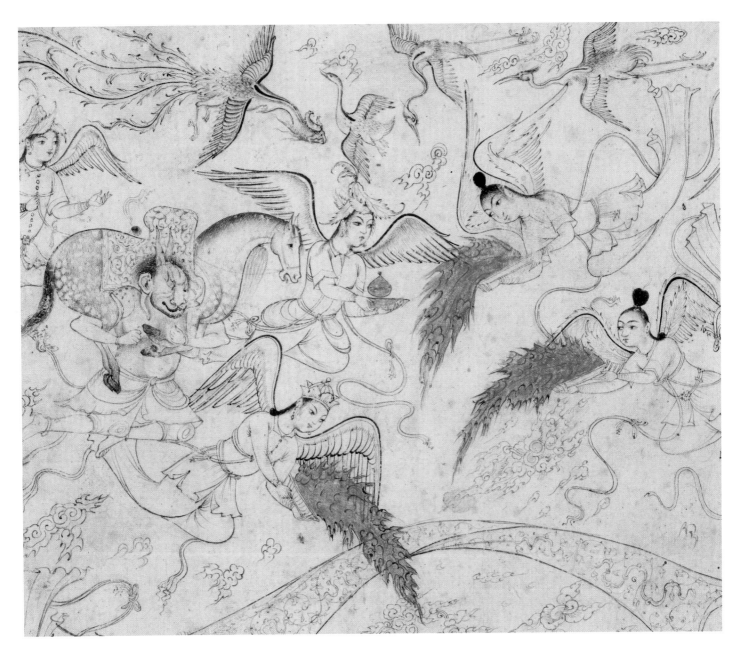

On the upper portion are more winged creatures: *peris* bear a plate of fruit, covered bowls or an incense burner; a *jinn* carries the king's horse on his shoulder; and three other angels pour celestial fire over the ruler. Real and fantastic birds, such as a crane and a phoenix, accompany the travelers.

This highly detailed scene is executed in black with gold used exclusively in the heavenly fire, on the throne, musical instruments and vessels; the throne and vessels are encrusted with red, blue and green gems. Soft washes of red enhance the hills in the foreground and define some of the

long ribbons tied around the torsos of the winged females.

The princely figure is identified as Süleyman, or King Solomon, who travels through the heavens on his flying throne accompanied by the animals and beasts of his legendary kingdom. The hoopie used by Solomon to send messages to Belkis, the Queen of Sheba, is seen on the upper right.

This particular drawing must have been extremely popular and served as the model for two paintings, one of which was made in Istanbul around 1600 and the other executed in Golconda in the

1680s.[36] The Freer drawing was formerly in an album belonging to the Ottoman Palace, which accounts for its Turkish copy.[37] However, it is difficult to trace the origin of the Indian rendition. Both paintings are so close to the Freer example, in size as well as in composition, that it is implausible to think of a second version which would have been used by the Golconda painter. It is more likely that the Indian painting was traced from the Turkish copy.

The Freer drawing is a product of the early Tabriz school, showing a blend of Timurid-Herat and Akkoyunlu-Tabriz styles.

13. Garden of Heavenly Creatures
Iran, Safavid period, mid-16th century

Black line, gold and silver on paper; tinted with red and blue
Page: 27.9 x 17.2 cm.
  (11 x 6¹³⁄₁₆ in.)
Drawing: 32.1 x 21.4 cm.
  (12⅝ x 8½ in.)
50.2

Similar to the previous drawing, this example is mounted on heavy paper with several gold lines framing the scene. It was also formerly in the imperial libraries of the Ottoman sultans.[38]

The scene depicts a garden with a group of *peris* entertaining their queen who is seated in a tree guarded by a *jinn.* A stream of water springs from the rocks in the middle of the scene and flows through the foot of the tree, cutting diagonally across the composition. This diagonal line is repeated by the steps leading to the tree house and balanced by the horizontal placement of the figures and the vertical thrust of the plane tree.

In the foreground are a pair of musicians playing a flute and tambourine and a dancer. Next to them are an amorous couple with an attendant who offers the lovers a cup of wine. Beyond the stream is a *jinn* leaning on a staff, guarding the entrance to the tree house. Several figures ascend the steps, carrying bowls of fruit and other delicacies; at the foot of the steps, one of the *peris* hands a bowl of fruit to an attendant. The queen of these heavenly creatures sits on the balustraded platform, leaning against a cushion; she is picking a fruit from a bowl offered by an attendant while another *peri,* sitting on one of the branches, plays a lute.

The platform and the two gates at the bottom and top of the stairs are adorned with delicate floral and geometric motifs. Similar intricate designs appear on the garments of the figures. The background is densely filled by the luxuriously foliated plane tree, blossoming branches, sprays of leaves and clusters of flowers; it is enriched by such details as birds perched on rocks or branches and softly falling leaves.

The paradisiacal garden is not entirely devoid of unpleasantness. On the upper right, a snake has attacked a bird's nest and is devouring one of the infants while the mother flutters helplessly above.

The scene is executed in crisp lines and washes of red and blue which soften the landscape and architectural elements. Gold is used on the metallic objects such as the vessels held by the *peris* and the jewelry of the *jinn* and on the cape of the dancer. The silver pigment applied to the stream has oxidized, appearing now as dark gray.

The exuberant landscape, jagged rocks and tall elegant figures suggest that the drawing belongs to the Kazvin school which flourished after Shah Tahmasp moved his court to that city in 1548.

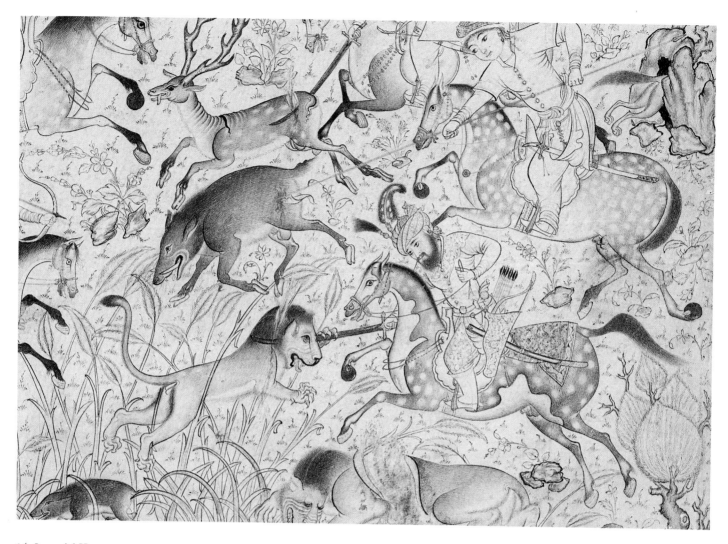

14. Imperial Hunt

Iran, Safavid period, mid-16th century

Black line, gold and silver on
  paper; tinted with red, blue
  and green
Page: 33.5 x 23.2 cm.
  (13³/₁₆ x 9⅛ in.)
Drawing: 30.3 x 20.4 cm.
  (11¹⁵/₁₆ x 8¹/₁₆ in.)
54.32

This tinted drawing is pasted on
an album sheet which is painted
beige with gold floral motifs
adorning the margins. On the
back there is an illuminated poem
written in *nastalik* and set in four
columns. Gold lines frame the
text and drawing on both sides of
the folio.

The scene depicts an imperial
hunt with nine riders about to
converge at the center, galloping
after their prey from opposite
sides of the folio. The extraordinary movement created by animals and men begins on the lower
portion and moves up the composition in a dynamic zigzag forma-
tion, each element counterbalanced by another.

In the foreground is a body of
water, its shore lined with rocks
and reeds. The princely hunter on
the lower right slashes the neck of
a lion with his sword while a
bleeding lion lies dying on the
ground. The prince is elaborately
dressed in embroidered garments
and bears a jeweled tassel and
feather in his turban. On the next
register, a hunter with a bow and
arrow shoots at a boar which is
speared by another rider. Behind
them, two hunters with swords
attack a stag and another pair of
riders chases onagers, trampling a
mountain goat. On the upper
right, a huntsman rushes to the
aid of a rider who is surprised by
two leopards; one leopard tears at
the horse and the other pounces
upon the rider.

The ferocious hunt is being observed by a bear who has escaped
to the safety of a tree and follows
the activity while wrapped around
a branch. Three figures appear
among the jagged and animated
mountains in the background; one
of them indicates his bewilder-
ment by the traditional gesture of
bringing an index finger to his
lips while pointing to the figure
aiming his musket on the wild
goats or sheep perched on the
craggy rocks.

While the hunters are rushing
after their kill, foxes and rabbits
scurry around, jump into crevices
in the rocks or peer cautiously out
of their dens, alerted by the
commotion.

Most of the drawing is executed
in black lines and washes. Occasional details of the landscape, a
few animals and portions of the
garments are rendered in pale red,
blue and green tints. Gold appears in the metal parts of the
weapons, horse trappings and
garments as well as on the
brocaded saddlecloth of the
prince; the eyes of the bear
perched on the tree are also
painted gold, stressing the creature's state of anxiety and fright.

On the lower left is a seal which is
too unclear to decipher. The
drawing is attributed to the Kazvin court and thought to belong
to the school of Sultan Muhammed, one of the most celebrated
artists of the age.

43

15. Dancing Sufis
Attributed to Muhammedi
Iran, Safavid period, ca. 1575

Black line and gold on paper;
  tinted with red
Page: 45 x 30.3 cm.
  (17¹¹⁄₁₆ x 11¹⁵⁄₁₆ in.)
Drawing: 15.2 x 11.1 cm.
  (6 x 4½ in.)
46.15

This folio represents the characteristic format of a page from a *murakka,* or album, in which select examples of paintings and drawings are combined with samples of calligraphy and illumination. Each page was carefully designed, the illustrations and text forming a harmonious and well-balanced composition. Single-page paintings or drawings were very popular in the 16th century and the compilation of albums became highly fashionable in the court. Signed works were particularly desirable and a great number of these albums include the best works of past and present painters and calligraphers.

This composite folio contains a drawing of dancing sufis, or mystics, by Muhammedi; a painting of a cluster of primroses by Murad; an unsigned text in prose, followed by a verse of poetry with an illuminated heading, both written in *nastalik*; a poem with five verses, written by Shah Mahmud in a fine *nastalik* script; and several strips of illuminated bands. The margins of the folio are tinted turquoise and adorned with gold motifs; gold and colored lines frame the illustrations, texts and illuminations which are enclosed by a scroll of gold arabesques. The seal on the drawing reads: "the slave of the King of Holiness (that is, Ali, the fourth caliph and the founder of the Shiite sect), Abbas, in the year 995 (1587)." The date on the seal must refer to the year in which the album was compiled, since the style of the drawing indicates that it was executed in Kazvin in the 1570s (see also no. 19A). Presently, the folio is mounted on a blank cardboard.

The poem with five verses, or 10 hemistichs, is written on an angle and follows the format of specimens of calligraphy executed for albums. The inscription, "the slave Shah Mahmud has written it," appears in a cartouche at the bottom. Shah Mahmud, a native of Nishapur, worked in the atelier of Shah Tahmasp and copied the most famous manuscripts of the century, including the celebrated *Haft Avrang* of Jami in the Freer Gallery of Art[39] and the *Khamsa* of Nizami in London.[40] The calligrapher, called "Zarin Kalam," or "Golden Pen," excelled in both large and small types of script and wrote a number of poems. He spent the latter part of his life composing poetry and working on calligraphy in Meshhed where he died in 1564.[41]

The painting of the primroses bears the inscription: "the work of Ustad (Master) Murad." Two artists with the name Murad, both of undistinguished fame, are associated with the Safavid court: Murad Daylami was in the atelier of Shah Tahmasp, and Murad ibn Ali was in the court of Shah Abbas.[42] It is more likely that this painting was made by the second artist.

The inscription on the drawing of the dancing sufis, written in the same hand as the one on the painting, states: "the work of Ustad Muhammedi Haravi," referring to Muhammedi who was from Herat. The attribution seems to be accurate since the same fine style of drawing and this same subject matter are found in other works reliably given to Muhammedi. The scene is executed in delicate lines with gold paint used exclusively in the floral sprays scattered around the ground and red washes reserved for the faces of the figures.

The 10 sufis are depicted in naturalistic and spontaneous poses, dancing in a circle to the rhythm of the tambourine played by the kneeling figure on the upper right. The figures are humorously represented, each doing his best, turning and swinging with raised arms. The three sufis on the top—a short stocky personage, a bearded middle-aged man and an elderly figure with a white beard—are portrayed with a marvelous sense of humor; the intense concentration of the first, the awkward pose of the second and the attempted agility of the third present excellent character studies. The others in the group are either beardless youths shown in three-quarter view or middle-aged men with prominent noses and chins drawn in profile.

Muhammedi, whose works were discussed earlier, was also a first-rate painter. His signature, rendered as "the work of Muhammed Haravi," appears on the portrait of a young Safavid prince (37.8, no. 15A) which once belonged to another album. The verso of this folio contains a sample of calligraphy executed by Muhammed Riza in 1574. The same round face with almond eyes and the tapered turban with a tall baton appear on the youthful sufis. The execution of the prince is highly polished, intentionally labored and refined in contrast to the lively youths in the drawing. The elaborately brocaded coat, adorned with scenes of warriors capturing prisoners, is a rare depiction of the famous figural textiles of the Safavid court.

15A. Portrait of a Young Prince
Signed by Muhammed Haravi
Iran, Safavid period, mid-16th century
(37.8)

16A. Camel and Keeper
Signed by Sheykh Muhammed
Iran, Safavid period, dated 1556-57
(37.21)

16. Prince with a Parakeet

Signed by Sheykh Muhammed
Iran, Safavid period, ca. 1575

Black line and gold on paper;
  tinted with red and green
Page: 15.7 x 9.2 cm.
  (6³⁄₁₆ x 3⅝ in.)
Drawing: 14.7 x 8.3 cm.
  (5¹³⁄₁₆ x 3¼ in.)
37.23

The drawing, mounted on heavy paper, has been cropped with red and gold borders added around the edges. The prince, set against an empty background, is shown kneeling, looking at the parakeet perched on his extended right hand. He is attired in the garments of the period with a striped turban wrapped around a soft feathery top and adorned with a single plume attached by a pin. He wears a long-sleeved shirt under a short-sleeved outfit tied at the waist with a sash; a striped handkerchief, a dagger and a penknife are tucked into the belt. In his left hand, the prince holds a pen.

The application of gold is reserved for the pin on the turban and for the metal parts of the pen. Red appears in the stripes of the handkerchief and turban as well as on the shirt, and is used in depicting the precious stones of the pin and earring. Green washes are applied to the feathery top of the turban, the sash and the parakeet.

The minute signature, barely visible below the tip of the penknife, reads: "drawing by Sheykh Muhammed." Its wording and placement are identical to a similar drawing in the Louvre.[43] In both works, the subjects have heavy eyelids, and the lines of the upper and lower lids project beyond the outline of the face.

The same features are present in Sheykh Muhammed's only dated painting which represents a camel with its keeper, enclosed by a poem related to the subject (37.21, no. 16A). The cartouche on the top, written in red, gives the date, 964 Hijra, or 1556-57 A.D.; the panel below, also executed in red, states: "*musavvir va muharrir* (painter and calligrapher, or writer) Sheykh Muhammed." The artist, who was the son of a calligrapher, obviously practiced both painting and the art of fine writing. The poem was most

likely written by him as a companion piece to his painting. It is executed in a fine gold *nastalik* script and pasted on an album sheet with additional verses and stripes of illumination adorning the edges. The precise line and harmonious color employed in this painting also appear in the illustrations attributed to Sheykh Muhammed in Shah Tahmasp's *Shahname* and Ibrahim Mirza's *Haft Avrang.*[44]

The theme of a figure seated in a kneeling position, holding various objects such as books, flowers or wine cups, was very popular in the Safavid period and frequently occurs in single-page drawings (nos. 19, 20, 32, 36 and 51).

17. Drinking Party

Iran, Safavid period, late 16th or
  early 17th century

Black line on paper; tinted with
  red, blue and yellow
16.3 x 10 cm. (6⁷⁄₁₆ x 3¹⁵⁄₁₆ in.)
40.18

The drawing, cropped to the edge
and pasted on cardboard, is
framed by thin gold, red and
black lines. It represents a group
of 10 figures who are seated or
standing in the foreground,
gathered around a large jar, over
which one of them is leaning. In
the background is a rich landscape
with articulated trees, shrubs and
rocks filling three-fourths of the
folio; on the upper right is a
domed brick structure with a tiled
entrance portal.

Red washes appear on the brick
facade of the structure, in the
bushes and rocks and on the long
stoles of the figures. The large jar
is decorated with blue and red
motifs while the tile panel on the
building has a blue floral scroll.
The dome of the structure is
painted yellow, suggesting a
golden shell.

The group consists of an assort-
ment of ages and types, including
dervishes and youths: two of the
men are bareheaded while the rest
of the figures wear a variety of
turbans and caps. Beardless
youths intermingle with older
men who have short or long
beards; some hold wine cups,
long-necked bottles or small
rounded fruit.

The figure leaning over the large jar is in a drunken stupor; his turban has fallen to the ground, its folds undone and dangling from his neck. He holds an unidentifiable object which looks like an animal's tail.

The ceramic jar resembles Chinese Ming dynasty wares, which were greatly in demand during this period. Shah Abbas had accumulated a large collection of Chinese porcelains which he donated in 1611 to the ancestral shrine of Sheykh Safi al-Din at Ardabil. The example in the drawing is extraordinarily large, and the red and blue decorations represent a rare type. It is possible that cer-

tain artistic liberties were taken in both the size and glaze of the immense jar, so as to exaggerate the amount of wine consumed by the party.

Drinking figures, alone or in groups, were frequently portrayed on single-page paintings and drawings by the Isfahan artists, representing the most popular pastime of the members of the court and the public (nos. 19, 20, 23, 30-32 and 36). This group, a mixture of layman, sufis and dervishes, participates in a common activity which takes place in the vicinity of one of the holy shrines scattered throughout Iran.

18. Musicians and Dancers
Attributed to Mirza Muhammed
al-Huseyni
Iran, Safavid period, dated 1613

Black line and gold on paper;
    tinted with red, blue, green
    and yellow
Page: 36 x 24.2 cm.
    (14⅛ x 9½ in.)
Drawing: 17.3 x 9.9 cm.
    (6¾ x 3⅞ in.)
07.157

The tinted drawing of five
figures—two of them dressed in
goatskins, dancing to the music
provided by a quartet—was originally a part of an album. It is
mounted on a pale green sheet
adorned with gold marginal decorations depicting flying geese,
roosters, butterflies and ducks in a
landscape. A gold floral scroll
frames the drawing with additional gold, red and green lines
encircling the border.

The back of the sheet has similar
marginal drawings with rabbits,
deer, foxes and butterflies surrounding four panels of text. Each
panel contains a couplet written
in white *nastalik* on brown or blue
ground. The date 1032 Hijra, or
1623 A.D., appears in the last
panel.

The drawing depicts the dancers
and musicians performing in a
landscape with a large tree and
several different types of bushes
rising above the rocks in the
background. The ground is
sprinkled with small rocks, clusters of grass and floral sprays. On
the upper right, two men with
long tapered hats surmounted by
animal tails dance in exaggerated
poses, swinging their arms and
jumping on one foot. Below is
another dancer in the same pose,
his long sleeves dangling over his
arms. He is flanked by two figures attired in goatskins and playing clappers. The four musicians
in the foreground perform with a
tambourine, panpipes and two
drums.

The scene is executed in black line
with gold applied sparingly to the
metal parts of the hats, musical
instruments and horns of the cos-
tumes. Soft washes of red, blue,
green and yellow appear in the
landscape and on the garments.

An inscription, added at a later period, states that the drawing was made by Mirza Muhammed al-Huseyni in 1012 Hijra, that is, 1613 A.D. The name of this artist is not found on any of the paintings or drawings of the period, nor is it recorded in the lists of calligraphers and painters pertaining to the 17th century.

Dancing figures wearing animal masks or skins appear in Islamic art, particularly during the Safavid period, and represent itinerant entertainers.[45] The composition and the grouping of figures seen in this drawing are based on an example in Leningrad which bears the signature of Muhammedi; another version of the same scene, also with Muhammedi's name, is in London, while a third is in a private collection.[46]

All four drawings employ the same group of musicians, the dancing pair wearing tall hats and the two men in animal skins. In the Leningrad example, the single dancer with dangling sleeves is placed on the top of the folio and another figure attired in goatskin is added to the center of the scene; in the London copy, the single dancer is omitted and one of the men clad in an animal skin is reversed; in the third version, there is an additional musician as well as another dancer. The Freer drawing is closer in composition to the Leningrad example, but the dancers are organized in a more structured manner, forming a semicircle leading to the musicians; the setting is more detailed with elaborate elements filling the landscape.

19. Youth with a Wine Cup

Signed by Riza-i Abbasi
Iran, Safavid period, early 17th
   century

Black line and gold on paper;
   tinted with magenta, blue
   and green
Page: 29.5 x 18.5 cm.
   (11⅜ x 7¼ in.)
Drawing: 13.5 x 8.9 cm.
   (5⁵⁄₁₆ x 3½ in.)
28.10

The drawing of a kneeling youth
offering a cup of wine is pasted on
an album leaf mounted on
cardboard. The leaf, tinted beige
and decorated with gold, depicts a
landscape with pairs of predators
and their prey—such as a lion and
gazelle, fox and goat and lion and
hare. The animals appear on the
top, right and bottom portions of
the folio; the left margin has been
trimmed to the edge of the drawing. The drawing is framed by a
series of gold, blue, green and
white lines around which is a
border of gold-speckled beige
paper, enclosed by additional gold
lines.

The youth wears a gold embroidered magenta cap with a blue
feathery top; his sash is striped in
green, blue and gold while a gold
collar and a series of gold buttons
adorn his garment. The landscape
elements—a willowy tree and
clusters of grass and flowers—are
rendered in gold, as are the shal-
low cup in his extended hand and
the tall-necked wine bottle on the
lower left. The signature, placed
along the lower edge, reads:
"drawing by Riza-i Abbasi."

The figure is placed firmly on the
ground, kneeling on a piece of
cloth. Arrested movement of this
type is rare among the single-
figure representations by the
artist.

Riza's single-page album paintings often portray aloof figures who seem to possess dream-like or other-worldly qualities. The same controlled line, soft modeling and drapery folds with crisp and agitated edges also appear in the two signed paintings by Riza owned by the Freer Gallery of Art (32.9 and 54.24, nos. 19A and 19B). The painting which portrays a young woman holding a fan is signed: "the work of Aka Riza" (no. 19A). The library seal of Shah Abbas with the date 1587, the year of his accession to the Safavid throne, appears on the portrait and helps to date the painting. This example, executed shortly after Riza joined the court of Shah Abbas, is probably one of his earliest works. The other painting represents a reclining nude wrapped in a diaphanous sheet; she has fallen asleep or is daydreaming at the edge of the water while reading a book of verses (no. 19B). The signature, written above her neatly placed slippers, reads: "the work of Riza." Both paintings, formerly in imperial albums, are mounted on folios adorned with illuminated bands or verses of poetry. Both the reclining nude and the portrait of the woman holding a fan, were made during the last two decades of the 16th century and predate the drawing of the kneeling youth with a wine cup by several years.

19A. Woman with a Fan
Signed by Aka Riza
Iran, Safavid period, ca. 1590
(32.9)

Riza's signatures have caused some confusion among scholars, since he uses "Riza," "Aka Riza" and "Riza-i Abbasi." It was generally believed that during the earlier part of his career he preferred "Riza," then changed to "Aka Riza" and finally, in homage to his patron, added "Abbasi" to his name. There has also been some discussion as to whether all three signatures actually belonged to the same artist. However, judging from the dated examples of Riza's work in the Freer album, it appears that he used different versions of his name without any chronological or logical sequence. For instance, both "Riza-i Abbasi" and "Aka Riza" are used on two examples made in 1639 (nos. 31 and 33).

Generally Riza's paintings bear the phrase *mashaka-hu*, "painted by," and his drawings are inscribed *rakimu-hu*, "drawn (or sketched) by." This is the case with the tinted drawing of the youth with a wine cup as well as with other examples included in the album (nos. 27-33). On these drawings he frequently uses the phrase *rakm-i kamina*, "drawn by the humble servant," which precedes his name.

19B. Reclining Nude
Signed by Riza
Iran, Safavid period, ca. 1590
(54.24)

20. Man with a Wine Cup
Signed by an anonymous follower
    of Riza
Iran, Safavid period, mid-17th
    century

Black line and gold on paper;
    tinted with blue
Page: 36.5 x 24 cm.
    (14⅜ x 9⁷⁄₁₆ in.)
Drawing: 11.4 x 8 cm.
    (4½ x 3¹⁄₁₆ in.)
07.2

The drawing of a kneeling man is
pasted on an album sheet which
has a poem of four lines enhanced
by delicate illumination on the
reverse. Written on an angle in a
fine *nastalik,* the verses are signed
by Hasan Shamlu.[47]

Each side of the folio is decorated
with gold marginal drawings on a
pink ground. The reverse depicts
a hawk hunting a goose on the
top while a fox chases a rabbit below; willowy trees and a hawk
adorn the sides.

The margins around the drawing
are filled with clusters of carna-
tions, tulips, hyacinths, irises and
primroses with butterflies and insects hovering around them. Blue
and gold lines are drawn around a
frame of scrolling gold leaves
which enclose the drawing and
the four lines of poetry.

The drawing, executed on brown
paper, shows a bearded man kneeling on the ground holding a wine
bottle and a cup with several pears
placed in front. Gold is applied to
the cup as well as to the clouds
and shrubs in the background.
The only other color in the scene
is blue which appears in the lining of the man's sleeve.

The inscription, placed above the
cup, is interpreted as: "copied by
the slave (or follower) of Riza-i
Abbasi." The figure represented
appears to be a dervish, wearing a
12-gored cap under his turban
and a long stole wrapped around
his shoulders. The poetry on the
top and bottom of the portrait refers to a *sheykh* who was once
averse to the pleasures of wine but
finally succumbed and became
boisterously drunk. Album folios
were often composed with paintings and poetry which expressed
similar sentiments, providing pictorial and verbal versions of the
same theme.

21. Old Man in a Landscape

Iran, Safavid period, early 17th century

Black line on paper; tinted with red
Page: 24.4 x 15.8 cm.
(9⅛ x 6¼ in.)
Drawing: 11.6 x 6.8 cm.
(4½ x 2⅝ in.)
67.7

This drawing, surrounded by a gold-flecked blue sheet and enclosed by several gold, blue and white lines, is mounted on blank cardboard. The figure is drawn in sharp and swiftly executed black lines while the landscape elements in the background are rendered with softer brush strokes. Touches of red appear only on the face of the old man, modeling his cheeks and defining his lips.

The figure is represented in an exaggerated position, leaning back against a tree trunk while extending his right hand. It is possible that this drawing is unfinished and the personage was meant to hold an object in his hand.

The technique and style of execution are very close to those of Riza; this scene was either sketched by him or made by one of his close followers.

22. Two Youths Embracing

Iran, Safavid period, mid-17th century

Black line on paper; tinted with red, blue, green and white
Page: 33.4 x 22.9 cm.
   (13⅛ x 9 in.)
Drawing: 22.9 x 13.9 cm.
   (9 x 5½ in.)
54.28

The back of this album leaf contains an illuminated quatrain written in *nastalik* by Muhammed Huseyin al-Tabrizi, the renowned calligrapher who was placed in charge of the inscriptions on government buildings and gates during the reign of Ismail II.[48] He is said to have taught calligraphy to Riza.

The tinted drawing is enclosed by thin red, blue, green and gold lines, with a wide yellow and red border added at a later date. It depicts two embracing youths, a subject with erotic implication not uncommon for the period. The arms of the youths are around each other, their embrace accentuated by the engulfing stoles. The intertwined branches of the tree in the background, the two different types of plants and a pair of bottles in the foreground can be interpreted as subtle references to the relationship of the youths.

A touch of red is added to the lips of the figure on the left; blue is applied to the lining of the garments, one of the wide sashes and the scalloped collar of the tall-necked bottle; green appears on the stole of the youth on the right. The use of white—on the headdress, shoes, stripes of the sash and the knife—is rather unusual and rarely occurs on the other drawings of the period. The cup held by one of the figures and the tall-necked bottle in the foreground are also rendered in white, suggesting that they are porcelain or high-fired wares.

23. Prince Seated on a Rock
Iran, Safavid period, 17th century

Black line and gold on paper
Page: 42 x 28.8 cm.
  (16½ x 11⅜ in.)
Drawing: 21 x 11.6 cm.
  (8¼ x 4⁹⁄₁₆ in.)
68.11

One side of this album leaf represents a youthful prince seated on a rock while the other contains a Mughal tinted drawing depicting lovers. The leaf is crudely designed with damaged strips of calligraphy pasted around a garish red and yellow border.

The prince is attired in the garments of Shah Tahmasp's reign with a tapered turban wound around a thin and tall cap. Two different types of feathers adorning the headdress and the richly embroidered coat suggest that the subject is of noble birth. The casual manner in which the prince sits—crossing his right leg over the other after having removed one shoe, his coat partially off with only one sleeve over his shoulder—also points to mid-16th century traditions, indicating that the drawing was copied from an earlier model. It is possible that the subject represents Shah Tahmasp himself.

The figure holds a wine bottle and cup, while watching an entertainer dressed in goatskin who dances and plays clappers. There is a tray of fruit in the background.

Gold is used to depict the landscape elements, and appears on the coat and such metallic portions of the figure's costume as the buttons, belt and jewelry on the turban. The vessels—wine bottle, cup and tray—are also rendered in gold.

24. Woman with a Large Jar
Signed by Muhammed Muhsin
Iran, Safavid period, dated 1649

Black line and gold on paper;
   tinted with red and blue
Page: 33 x 21.7 cm.
   (13 x 8⁹⁄₁₆ in.)
Drawing: 21.1 x 10.1 cm.
   (8⁵⁄₁₆ x 4 in.)
12.99

The margins of this folio are decorated with arabesques containing
animal heads and cartouches sten-
ciled in red on a blue ground. The
leaf, mounted on blank cardboard, contains two gold-flecked
stripes placed on either side of the
drawing.

The illustration represents a
young woman carrying a large
single-handled jar, swaying ele-
gantly under its weight. An
elaborately knotted sash encircles
her waist while a long stole
wrapped around her torso ripples
behind. Her dress is embroidered
with gold cloud motifs. Gold is
also used on an ornament hanging
on her forehead and in the tree,
clouds, clusters of grass and blossoms adorning the background.
Touches of red appear in the
woman's beaded necklace, shoes
and undergarment, while blue is
added to the lining and buttons of
her dress and to the stripes in her
sash. The jar, inspired by Chinese
porcelains, is decorated with a
blue branch around which a pair
of red-winged birds fly. The scalloped ring around the neck and
the fancy handle suggest that the
artist took certain liberties in representing a Ming dynasty ware
(see also no. 17).

The inscription on the upper right
of the composition reads: "drawing by Muhammed Muhsin,"
below which is the date 1059
Hijra, or 1649 A.D. An identical
drawing, bearing the same date,
was recently sold in London.[49] It
seems remarkable that the artist
executed two versions of the scene
in the same year. Drawings by
this artist are extremely rare; the
only other known example is included in the exhibition (no. 25).

25. Dervish and His Disciple
Signed by Muhammed Muhsin
Iran, Safavid period, mid-17th
century

Black line on paper; tinted with
red, blue and yellow
Page: 19.3 x 12 cm.
(7⅝ x 4¹¹⁄₁₆ in.)
Drawing: 16.8 x 9.3 cm.
(6⅝ x 3⅝ in.)
47.23

The second drawing bearing the
name of Muhammed Muhsin is
mounted on blank cardboard and
framed with pink and beige
panels adorned with gold motifs.
The finely drawn scene represents
a bearded dervish seated at the
foot of a tree, smoking a water
pipe held by a youthful disciple.
A body of water ripples in the
foreground, its shore lined with
rocks and vegetation. The luxuriously foliated tree gracefully extends to the upper portion of the
folio with decorative clouds and
birds filling the background.

Washes of red appear in the tree
trunk, the disciple's cap, the
water pipe, and on the sheet
below the dervish; blue is used on
the youth's garment and in the
dervish's hat; yellow appears on
the disciple's stole and scarf,
around his master's hat and in the
leaves of the tree.

The inscription, placed in the
center of the drawing, next to the
tree, reads "Muhammed Muhsin."
Although there is some difference
in the style of writing of this signature as compared with that on
the previous example, the execution of the clouds and birds and of
the folds and ripples in the stoles
worn by the figures in both works
support the attribution to
Muhammed Muhsin.

26. Monkey Riding a Lion
Signed by Muin Musavvir
Iran, Safavid period, dated 1672

Black line on paper; tinted with
    red and yellow
Page: 22.5 x 16.2 cm.
    (8⅞ x 6⅜ in.)
Drawing: 13.5 x 7 cm.
    (5⅜ x 2¾ in.)
66.13

Muin Musavvir, the most talented
follower of Riza, was as prolific a
painter as his master. His drawings reveal an excellent control of
line and an interest in original
subject matter. This example,
which represents a trained monkey riding a tame lion, is
mounted on a blank cardboard
with unattractive red and blue
borders added at a later date.

The monkey wears a pointed yellow cap and carries a banner and a
shield tinted red. Red also appears
on the tongue of the lion strolling
in the landscape. The lengthy inscription placed on an angle across
the top of the drawing reads: "on
Wednesday, the 4th of the month
of Shavval, in the propitious year
1082 (February 3, 1672), this was
drawn for an album, Muin
Musavvir (that is, Muin, the
painter) drew it, may God forgive
him, may it be auspicious." The
wording and precise dating are
consistent with the inscriptions
found on contemporary drawings
(see nos. 27-46).

This drawing was executed during
the middle of Muin's career
which, according to known dated
examples, spanned the years between 1635 and 1707. One of his
earliest works, dated 1638, is also
included in the exhibition
(no. 34).

This example, rendered in an extremely free and lively manner, is
one of his best drawings. It depicts a unique subject in which
trained animals were used by entertainers, falling into the same
genre depicted in numbers 18
and 23.

27. Man Scratching His Head
From the *Riza-i Abbasi Album*
Signed by Riza
Iran, Safavid period, dated 1598

Black line on paper
11.7 x 7 cm. (4⅝ x 2¾ in.)
53.12

One of Riza's earliest drawings represents a man who has removed his large turban and is scratching his head in a preoccupied manner. The figure, portrayed with earthy naturalism and humor, is attired in a long garment held at the waist by a wide sash.

The long inscription states that it was made: "in Meshhed, at end of Friday, 10th of Muharrem, 1007 (August 14, 1598) for Mirza Khojegi, in his house, by Riza." Single-page drawings commissioned by wealthy citizens often have similar lengthy comments inscribed by the artists, giving the precise date and place of execution.

This example was made under the most auspicious circumstances: in the city of Meshhed, venerated for its holy shrines; during Muharrem, the most sacred month of the year; and on Friday, the day of rest and worship for the Muslims. The patron, Mirza Khojegi, was probably a highly devout person, and the figure most likely represents one of the Meshhed pilgrims.

28. Puzzle Drawing of Horses
From the *Riza-i Abbasi Album*
Signed by Riza-i Abbasi
Iran, Safavid period, dated 1616

Black line on paper
12 x 15.4 cm. (4¾ x 6⅟₁₆ in.)
53.23

Puzzle sketches of two horses joined so as to represent two pairs were popular during the 17th century. The inscription at the bottom of the sheet is written in a style which differs from the handwriting found on Riza's other drawings. It reads: "9th of Shavval, 1025 (October 20, 1616), by Riza-i Abbasi."

Two later inscriptions added to the right margin can be partially deciphered and contain the name of a former owner, Mirza Abu'l-Kasim, and the date 1297 Hijra, or 1879 A.D. This information is quite significant, since it indicates that the ablum could not have been compiled before that date.

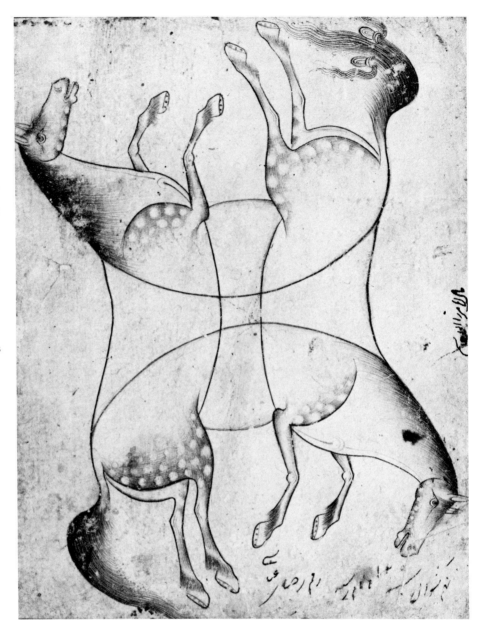

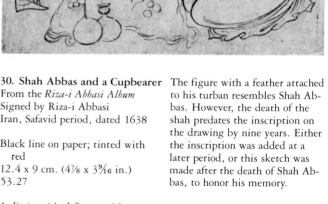

29. Man with a Spindle
From the *Riza-i Abbasi Album*
Signed by Riza-i Abbasi
Iran, Safavid period, dated 1633

Black line on paper; tinted with
   red, mauve and green
11.6 x 6.2 cm. (4⁹⁄₁₆ x 2⁷⁄₁₆ in.)
53.25

The tinted drawing represents a
man wearing a fur-brimmed hat
and baggy pants, spinning thread
from a piece of wool wrapped
around his arm. His hat and pants
are tinted green, the wool and
spool of thread are painted red,
and the fur brim on his headdress
is rendered in mauve.

The inscription on the right half
of the sheet states that the drawing was made: "on Saturday, 11th
of Rajab, 1042 (January 22,
1633), for a renowned physician
named Shamsa, 'the Galen of his
time,' by Riza-i Abbasi."

The outlines of the figure are perforated, suggesting that it was
used as a stencil. It is highly unlikely that a finished drawing,
specifically commissioned by a
physician, would have been used
as a stencil. It is possible that the
perforations were done at a later
date, after the drawing had
changed hands.

30. Shah Abbas and a Cupbearer
From the *Riza-i Abbasi Album*
Signed by Riza-i Abbasi
Iran, Safavid period, dated 1638

Black line on paper; tinted with
   red
12.4 x 9 cm. (4⅞ x 3⁹⁄₁₆ in.)
53.27

A distinguished figure with a
long drooping mustache sits in a
kneeling position next to a tree;
in front of him is a piece of fabric
with fruit, tall-necked bottles and
jars. A youthful attendant pours
wine from a bottle into a small
cup, ready to offer it to the seated
personage. The scene is executed
in black line with red applied
only to the turban of the main
figure. The inscription states that
the drawing was made on:
"Wednesday, 10th of Safar, 1048
(June 23, 1638), by Riza-i
Abbasi."

The figure with a feather attached
to his turban resembles Shah Abbas. However, the death of the
shah predates the inscription on
the drawing by nine years. Either
the inscription was added at a
later period, or this sketch was
made after the death of Shah Abbas, to honor his memory.

31. Youth Filling Wine Bottles
From the *Riza-i Abbasi Album*
Signed by Riza-i Abbasi
Iran, Safavid period, dated 1639

Black line on paper
13.5 x 10.6 cm. (5⁵⁄₁₆ x 4³⁄₁₆ in.)
53.28

The drawing depicting a youth filling a bottle from a large wine jar contains two inscriptions. On the upper right is a statement which reads: "drawing by the humble Riza-i Abbasi"; the other, on the bottom, states that it was: "made on the night leading to the 8th of Ramazan, 1048 (January 12-13, 1639)."

The scene was rapidly sketched and depicts a variety of jars and bottles together with a bowl of fruit placed at the foot of a tree; rocks and vegetation cover the ground while decorative clouds appear in the sky. The *saki,* or cupbearer, rests the single-handled large jar on his knee, pouring its contents into a funnel placed on the lip of one of the bottles. The figure wears a large turban with crisp folds and two curly locks fall on either side of his face. He is characteristic of the type of youth frequently represented in Riza's drawings.

The jar has a scalloped ring around the neck and is decorated with a branch and two birds, similar to the one seen in number 24.

32. Man with a Large Turban
From the *Riza-i Abbasi Album*
Signed by Riza-i Abbasi
Iran, Safavid period, mid-17th
  century

Black and red lines on paper
16 x 8.7 cm. (6⁵⁄₁₆ x 3⁷⁄₁₆ in.)
53.29

A beardless figure with a large
turban sits in a kneeling position,
surrounded by sketchy landscape
elements—including rocks, clusters of flowering shrubs and scalloped clouds. He has a wine cup
in one hand and holds a fruit in
the other.

Black line is used on the figure
and the inscription, while the setting is rendered in brownish red.
The inscription, almost hidden
amidst the shrubs and rocks on
the right, states that the drawing
was made by: "the humble Riza-i
Abbasi."

33. Camp Scene
From the *Riza-i Abbasi Album*
Signed by Aka Riza
Iran, Safavid period, dated 1639

Black line on paper
12.8 x 7.8 cm. (5⅟₁₆ x 3⅟₁₆ in.)
53.34

This detailed depiction of a nomadic camp shows a tent with a woman spinning wool in the foreground; a donkey with a camel and a man with a child are partially visible behind the tent. An older figure wearing a fur-lined coat and hat converses with a rider in the background while another man carries a large bowl next to the tree on the upper left.

The inscription across the top of the folio states that the drawing was made by Aka Riza for the treasury of his "Highness," which must refer to Shah Safi I who ruled between 1629 and 1642. The second inscription, on the upper left, gives the date: "Wednesday, 5th of Shavval, 1048 (February 9, 1639)."

This scene is the only one in the album with an inscription specifically stating that it was made for the court.

34. Portrait of a Youth
From the *Riza-i Abbasi Album*
Signed by Muina
Iran, Safavid period, dated 1638

Black line on paper; tinted with
  red
11.6 x 8.4 cm. (4⁹⁄₁₆ x 3⁵⁄₁₆ in.)
53.57

This portrait, executed on Friday,
the 20th of Ramazan, 1047 (February 5, 1638), in the house of a
nobleman whose name could not
be deciphered, is the only one in
the album by Muin Musavvir,
who has signed the drawing as
"Muina." It is one of the earliest
works of the artist whose name
appears on two other drawings
from the same collection (nos. 37
and 44).

Muin was the most talented of
Riza's students. He executed a
number of manuscript illustrations as well as single-page drawings and paintings during his
long career which spanned the
period from the 1630s to the first
decade of the 18th century.

The portrait is drawn in black line
with red tints applied to the subject's lips, cap and striped undershirt; a red line also accentuates
the contour of his torso.

35. Singing Bird
From the *Riza-i Abbasi Album*
Iran, Safavid period, dated 1619

Black line on paper
8.7 x 14.7 cm. (3⁷⁄₁₆ x 5¹³⁄₁₆ in.)
53.24

The inscription covering the left half of the drawing states that it was made on: "Friday, 2nd of Zu'l-Kada, 1028 (October 1, 1619), in the house of 'the Galen of his time,' the physician Saifa, by his order. . . ." The remaining words could not be read.

The wording is similar to that found on the drawing of a man spinning thread, also made for a physician called "the Galen of his time" (no. 29). Obviously, medical practitioners of the period were wealthy enough to afford the works of popular artists.

This example depicts a small bird perched on rocks from which sprays of weeds grow. The bird's open beak suggests the artist intended to illustrate a bird in the midst of song. Similar long-tailed birds with parted beaks appear on several other drawings from the same album (nos. 45, 56, 57 and 58).

36. Youth with a Wine Bottle
From the *Riza-i Abbasi Album*
Iran, Safavid period, dated 1638

Black line on paper
16.3 x 9.4 cm. (6⅞6 x 3¹¹⁄₁₆ in.)
53.26

A youth holding a tall-necked wine bottle extends a small cup while kneeling on the ground; a spray of branches decorates the background. The youth wears a soft feathery hat and has a flower tucked into his wide sash. The exaggerated drapery on the edges of his cuffs and hem, the articulated folds of his sash and the cloth beneath his knees are characteristic of the brushwork of the Isfahan school.

The inscription on the left has been partially deciphered and states that this drawing was made on Friday, the ninth of Muharrem, 1048 (May, 1638), in the orchard of a personage whose name could not be read. The date is confusing, since Friday was the seventh day of Muharram. Either the inscription was added at a later time, or the artist confused the date, which is a common human error.

37. Seated Man (top)
   Reclining Man (bottom)
From the *Riza-i Abbasi Album*
Iran, Safavid period, dated 1639

Black line on paper
Top: 11.8 x 6.9 cm.
   (4⅝ x 2¾ in.)
Bottom: 6.2 x 11.9 cm.
   (2⁷⁄₁₆ x 4¹¹⁄₁₆ in.)
53.30

The two drawings, executed on varying tones of paper by two different hands, are mounted on the same folio. The example on the top depicts a bearded man in a landscape with sheets of paper, a pair of bowls and his spectacles lying on the ground. It is pasted sideways on the page.

The drawing on the lower half of the folio is far more refined and represents a bareheaded, barefooted man reclining against a tree stump. His hair and beard are untrimmed and his clothes are slightly unkempt. He holds a cane in his hand and is gazing wearily into blank space. The inscription above the figure states that the drawing was made on: "Friday, 15th of Safar, 1049 (June 17, 1639), in the domain of my brother's shelter, Aka Muina." The wording of the inscription suggests that the drawing was made in the house of Muin Musavvir.

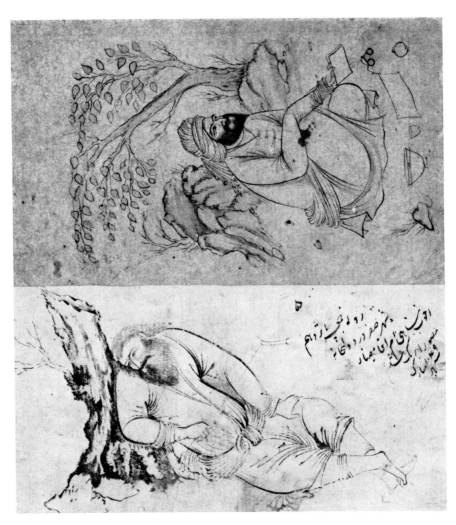

38. Sketch for *Layla va Majnun*
From the *Riza-i Abbasi Album*
Iran, Safavid period, dated 1639

Black line on paper
13.1 x 7.7 cm. (5³⁄₁₆ x 3¹⁄₁₆ in.)
53.33

The album contains several
sketches made for manuscript
illustrations, among which is this
example depicting an episode
from Nizami's love story of Layla
and Majnun. The scene shows the
emaciated Majnun conversing
with his uncle while surrounded
by the wild and tame animals
which befriended him in the wil-
derness. The incomplete drawing
of two rabbits on the lower left
suggests that the work was not
finished. There are several
purplish stains on the paper.

The inscription on the upper left
reads: "on Thursday, on the 6th of
Shavval, in the year 1048 (February 10, 1639), this was made."

39. Mughal Official (left)
   Seated Man (right)
From the *Riza-i Abbasi Album*
Iran, Safavid period, dated 1641

Black and red lines on paper;
   tinted with green and white
Left: 9.9 x 6.7 cm.
   (3¹⁵⁄₁₆ x 2⅝ in.)
Right: 9.7 x 7.1 cm.
   (3¹³⁄₁₆ x 2¹³⁄₁₆ in.)
53.14

The drawing on the left represents a Mughal official standing with his arms extended. The figure, drawn in black, wears the traditional garments of the Indian court. The inscription states that the drawing was made on Tuesday, 12th of Shavval, 1050 (January, 1641). Either the day of the week or the date is incorrect, since Tuesday fell on the ninth or 16th of Shavval in 1050 Hijra. The same inconsistency occurs on two other inscriptions (nos. 36 and 40). This personage possibly represents Khan Alam, who was sent by Jahangir to the court of Shah Abbas in 1618-19.

The other drawing is executed in red with green washes used in the turban and in the lining of the coat and pants; the handkerchief lying across the figure's lap is painted white. The roguish-looking man is shown seated with his wrists crossed, almost as if bound and imprisoned.

40. Old Man Holding a Staff
From the *Riza-i Abbasi Album*
Iran, Safavid period, dated 1641

Black line on paper
10.8 x 7.3 cm. (4¼ x 2⅞ in.)
53.39

According to the inscription, this
drawing was made on Tuesday,
the 12th of Shavval, 1050 (January, 1641), after an Indian work.
As in the previous inscription, the
statement contains an inconsistency between the day of the week
and the date of the month, Tuesday being the ninth or 16th of
Shavval.

It is difficult to imagine the "Indian" model that was used for this
portrait, since the figure type, the
costume and the style of execution
are characteristic of the mid-
17th-century school of Isfahan.

41. Lovers
From the *Riza-i Abbasi Album*
Iran, Safavid period, dated 1642

Black line on paper
13.2 x 6.8 cm. (5³⁄₁₆ x 2¹¹⁄₁₆ in.)
53.41

One of the finest drawings in the
album represents a handsome
couple, executed in soft but controlled lines. The man has a long
drooping mustache and wears the
turban of the age; his consort
wears a small cap tied at the back
and a thin ring on her nostril.
The harmonious relationship of
the figures reflect their emotional
attachment.

The extremely sketchy inscription
above the figures is partially read-
able and states that the drawing
was made "in the night of Thursday, 11th of Muharrem, 1052
(April 9-10, 1642), in a lane
(?) . . ."; the identification of the
location could not be established.

42. Polo Player

From the *Riza-i Abbasi Album*
Iran, Safavid period, dated 1642

Black and red lines on paper;
   tinted with purple, blue and
   green
15.7 x 10.3 cm. (3 3/16 x 4 1/16 in.)
53.44

There are several tinted drawings
in the album which indicate that
they were finished products. This
scene represents a polo player rendered in full color, galloping on a
lively horse with craggy rocks,
tree stumps and bushes rising on
the horizon. A group of rocks
with foliated plants appears in the
foreground while rippled clouds
decorate the sky. A feeling of
depth is created by the position of
the horse and rider; they are
shown from the back, turning
into the picture in a spiral
movement.

The young rider wears a fur-
brimmed cap and a green outfit
lined with blue. Black and red
lines are used interchangeably: the
latter are employed to draw the
landscape elements in the background as well as the outlines of
the horse.

The inscription above the rocks
merely states that the drawing
was made in the middle of Shaban, 1052 (November, 1642).

43. Wolf Hunter
From the *Riza-i Abbasi Album*
Iran, Safavid period, dated 1642

Black and red lines on paper
8.7 x 16.6 cm. (3⁷⁄₁₆ x 6⁹⁄₁₆ in.)
53.45

Similar to the previous drawing, this scene depicts a galloping rider in a landscape. The figure moves horizontally across the picture frame, shooting at two rather unperturbed wolves partially hidden behind the rocks. The rider wears a fur-brimmed hat and twists into the picture, his torso shown from the back. An embroidered quiver hangs from his side while two arrows are stuck in his belt.

The drawing is executed in black brush strokes with red lines used exclusively on the horse.

In contrast to the other inscriptions found in the album, this date is written out and given in digits: "on Friday, 27th of Shaban, thousand and fifty-two, 1052 (November 22, 1642)."

44. Shepherd in the Mountains
From the *Riza-i Abbasi Album*
Iran, Safavid period, dated 1643

Black line on paper; tinted with
    polychrome colors
6 x 10.5 cm. (2⅜ x 4⅛ in.)
53.48

The minuscule scene depicts a
weary shepherd seated on a rock,
resting against a rugged mountain; his dog lies at the foot of a
tree while several goats and sheep
peer over a hill. The artist has
drawn the forms with great deli-
cacy and made extensive use of
colored washes in the landscape
and on the figure. The hues are
quite extensive, including various
tones of red, blue, green, mauve,
brown and gray.

The inscription has been partially
deciphered and reads: "on Saturday, 16th of Rabi II, on that day
said (?) Muina . . . and thus this
drawing was made in the year
1053." The date given corresponds to July 4, 1643. The
casual and narrative manner in
which the date is rendered is
characteristic of 17th-century
inscriptions.

45. Old Man with a Cane
From the *Riza-i Abbasi Album*
Iran, Safavid period, mid-17th
  century

Black line on paper
13.5 x 5.6 cm. (5⁵⁄₁₆ x 2³⁄₁₆ in.)
53.16

This portrait of an elderly man
wearing a voluminous turban and
a long coat is an excellent character study. The face is highly ex-
pressive with twinkling eyes and a
benevolent smile. The figure
stands in front of a high hill with
rocks, plants and a solitary bird
added to the background.

According to the inscription on
the lower left, the drawing was
made in Herat on the 10th of
Safar; the year of execution is
omitted.

81

46. Two Hunters with a Falcon
From the *Riza-i Abbasi Album*
Iran, Safavid period, mid-17th
century

Red line on bluish-green paper;
  tinted with blue and yellow
13.4 x 21.7 cm. (5⁵⁄₁₆ x 8⁹⁄₁₆ in.)
53.46

A dramatic movement is created
by the two riders who gallop towards the stream, their horses and
fierce falcon arousing a group of
cranes. The sweeping movement
of men, horses and birds is coun-
teracted by an articulated tree
which curves gracefully over the
scene, creating a revolving and
self-contained composition.

One of the hunters is a middle-
aged man with a mustache and a
short beard; he wears a split-
brimmed hat and carries a quiver
filled with arrows. The other is a
younger figure who wears a feath-
ered cap and holds the string of a
flying decoy. The ferocious hawk
swoops down on its prey; five of
the cranes have been alerted and
hurriedly take flight while two
others still paddle in the water.

The scene is full of details accentuating the movement, such as
trailing clouds and softly bent
branches which follow the direction of the riders. In spite of a
multitude of elements, the scene
is spaciously and carefully
composed.

The use of tinted paper is rather
unusual although red lines were
used on other examples in the
album (nos. 48 and 57).

Similar to the legend on the previous drawing, this inscription
gives only the day and omits the
year: "Monday, 10th of Shaban."

47. Man with Spectacles (left)
 Shafi al-Abbasi (right)
From the *Riza-i Abbasi Album*
Iran, Safavid period, mid-17th
 century

Black line on paper; tinted with
 red; white lead applied for
 corrections
Left: 10.8 x 8.3 cm.
 (4¼ x 3⁵⁄₁₆ in.)
Right: 10.4 x 6 cm.
 (4⅛ x 2⅜ in.)
53.17

The drawing on the left is a remarkable study of a slightly over-
weight elderly man who wears
spectacles and holds a pad under
his arm. The sketch was corrected
with white lead which has discol-
ored and appears as dark gray.
This technical feature is also
found on a number of other drawings included in the album. The
corrected and original lines of certain parts of the figure are still
visible, especially in the hands
and legs.

The accompanying drawing represents a seated youth, resting his
drawing pad on his knee; working
with a fine brush, he is painting a
flower. Red is applied to the fur-
brimmed hat of the young artist
as well as to the petals of his
flower.

The inscription on the sheet with
the old man identifies the young
artist as "Shafi al-Abbasi."
Muhammed Shafi Abbasi was
Riza's son and excelled in the
painting of flowers.

It has been suggested that the
drawing of the old man is a self-
portrait of Riza who also executed
the portrait of his son.

48. Old Man Leaning on a Staff
From the *Riza-i Abbasi Album*
Iran, Safavid period, mid-17th
  century

Red line on paper
11.6 x 7.9 cm. (4⁹⁄₁₆ x 3⅛ in.)
53.40

This unfinished drawing portrays
a bearded man in a landscape, his
hands held high as if leaning on a
staff which has been omitted.

The fine brushwork in the representation of the figure and the
hills in the background suggest
that the artist was a close follower
of Riza. His indebtedness to his
teacher's brushwork is particularly
noticeable in the agitated strokes
around the edges of the stole and
the turban.

49. Dervish with a Cat
From the *Riza-i Abbasi Album*
Iran, Safavid period, mid-17th
  century

Black line on paper
9.2 x 5.1 cm. (3⅜ x 2 in.)
53.31

This drawing, which depicts a
dervish seated in front of a tree
with a large cat perched on his
back, characterizes the production
of the school of Isfahan. The
bearded figure wears a rounded
cap under his turban and a long-
sleeved garment, the cuffs of
which extend over his hands. Two
bowls and several pieces of fruit
appear in the foreground.

The dervish bends over under the
weight of the cat; his movement
is counterbalanced by the tree
trunk which extends in the opposite direction and is repeated by
the barren branches. The rounded
mass of the figure is contrasted by
the sketchy and linear execution
of the background.

50. Hunchback with a Bowl
From the *Riza-i Abbasi Album*
Iran, Safavid period, mid-17th
  century

Black line on paper
10.8 x 6.7 (4¼ x 2⅝ in.)
53.32

The drawing portrays a bearded
hunchback who struggles with a
large bowl, straining to lift it. By
placing the image against an
empty background, the artist accentuated the pathos of the de-
formed figure who has reconciled
himself to hardship and has ac-
cepted his fate.

Riza and his followers frequently
executed studies of humble
workmen and poor people, reflecting a social strata which differed
considerably from the upper
classes.

51. Young Man Holding Flowers
From the *Riza-i Abbasi Album*
Iran, Safavid period, mid-17th
   century

Black line on paper
15.1 x 8.5 cm. (5 15/16 x 3 3/8 in.)
53.22

This example represents an elegant courtier, wearing an elaborate turban adorned with feathers and attired in a coat embroidered with animals and landscape motifs. The figure kneels on the ground and holds a spray of flowers. A tapered penknife hangs from his sash into which a handkerchief is tucked.

This type of pose was almost a formula used by artists in portraying the young dandies of the court. Similar single-page drawings and paintings were executed in the 16th century and continued to be produced up to the end of the Safavid period (nos. 16, 19, 20 and 32).

52. Cloth Merchant
From the *Riza-i Abbasi Album*
Iran, Safavid period, mid-17th
    century

Black line on paper
17.1 x 11.5 cm. (6¾ x 4⁹⁄₁₆ in.)
53.43

In addition to representing
workmen, shepherds, wandering
dervishes and courtly figures, the
drawings of the Isfahan school also
portray the wealthy middle
classes. This crisply drawn example depicts a bearded merchant
kneeling on a carpet, holding a
length of cloth. Other pieces of
fabric lie on the ground together
with the tools of the merchant's
trade—a pair of scissors, a pen
case and inkwell, several sheets of
paper and some reed pens.

The varying thickness of line
lends a feeling of weight and volume to the figure; rapidly executed strokes define the drapery
and present a contrast between the
volumes and voids in the composition. The brush strokes on the
turban, shawl, cuffs and samples
of cloth are particularly well rendered, revealing the hand of a
highly competent artist.

53. Old Man Riding a Zebu

From the *Riza-i Abbasi Album*
Iran, Safavid period, mid-17th
   century

Black line on paper
12.2 x 9.9 cm. (4¹³⁄₁₆ x 3⅞ in.)
53.13

One of the most outstanding
drawings in the album represents
a bearded man riding a zebu. The
figure is executed in soft and delicate strokes which present only
the essential parts of the form.
Similar rapidly applied strokes define the animal and the landscape
in the background.

The bulky animal striding at a
slow pace and the elderly figure
bent with age are portrayed with
sensitivity as well as naturalism.
The scene projects timelessness
and harmony among man, beast
and nature.

88

54. Woman with Flowers (left)
   Woman with a Scarf (right)
From the *Riza-i Abbasi Album*
Iran, Safavid period, mid-17th
   century

Black line on paper
Left: 8 x 7.1 cm. (3⅛ x 2¹³⁄₁₆ in.)
Right: 6.1 x 5.6 cm.
   (2⁷⁄₁₆ x 2³⁄₁₆ in.)
53.58

The two studies of women are
very close in style and were possibly executed by the same hand.
The sketch on the left represents a
young woman holding flowers;
her flowing tresses are partially
covered with a cap which has a
peaked front and ribbons at the
back; her dress has a low collar
exposing an undershirt and several
beaded necklaces.

In the companion drawing the
head of the woman is covered
with a cap worn over a scarf with
locks of hair framing her face; a
pin adorns the cap. A flower is
tucked into the headdresses of
both ladies.

The figures represent the ideal
female beauty of the age, with a
round face, small puckered lips
and almond-shaped eyes framed
by heavy eyebrows which join together at the bridge of the
straight nose.

55. Old Man and Youth

From the *Riza-i Abbasi Album*
Iran, Safavid period, mid-17th
century

Black line on paper
12.2 x 12.6 cm. (4¹³⁄₁₆ x 5 in.)
53.42

Among the works of the period
are several drawings with erotic
implications and earthy humor of
the type which were favored by
Riza. This sketch represents a
lecherous old man making an in-
decent and highly suggestive gesture to a youth. The ground between the personages is filled with
rapidly executed rocks, clusters of
leaves, flowers and fruit.

The incomplete head of a man
which appears in the middle of
the scene must be a later addition;
his wide-eyed and startled expression is possibly meant to be a
comment on the assignation that
is about to take place.

56. Rider with Decapitated Enemy
From the *Riza-i Abbasi Album*
Iran, Safavid period, mid-17th
  century

Black line on paper
9.6 x 15.8 cm. (3³⁄₁₆ x 6¼ in.)
53.47

This example, with fine perforations following the outlines of the
drawing, was used as a stencil.
The drawing depicts a mounted
warrior leading a horse over which
the body of his slain enemy is
thrown. The warrior is in full ar-
mor: he wears an elaborate helmet
decorated with a plume and banner, carries his shield and weapons
on his back and holds a long spear
on top of which is the severed
head of the enemy.

The hills and vegetation in the
background imply that the scene
takes place in a mountainous and
wooded area. The two pairs of
oversized birds on the left seem
out of place and must have been
added later. This type of bird is
depicted on several other folios
of the album (nos. 35, 45, 57
and 58).

57. Landscape with Animals
From the *Riza-i Abbasi Album*
Iran, Safavid period, mid-17th
  century

Black and red lines on paper
18.4 x 8.3 cm. (7¼ x 3⁵⁄₁₆ in.)
53.35

The densely packed scene depicts
a variety of wild animals and birds
peacefully coexisting in nature. In
the foreground, a couple of wild
goats drink from the stream in
which ducks and fish swim. Behind them are a pair of foxes and a
family of lions with the female
suckling one cub while playing
with the other. A number of birds
are perched in the branches of the
two trees on the lower right and
upper left with more swooping
down from the sky.

The animals are drawn in black
and the landscape elements are
rendered in red. The birds on the
lower and upper right portion appear to have been corrected using
red over black lines. The drawing
may have been a sketch for a
painting, similar to the next
example.

58. Landscape with Animals
From the *Riza-i Abbasi Album*
Iran, Safavid period, mid-17th
century

Black and red lines on paper
18.8 x 9.4 cm. (7⅜ x 3¹¹⁄₁₆ in.)
53.36

This drawing, which also represents animals in a landscape, has been pierced and was used in stenciling. In contrast to the previous example, the scene contains fewer animals shown in combat. A fox in the foreground has caught a terrified crane by its legs while its mate dives down to attack the intruder. The movements of the cranes—one trying to ascend whereas the other descends—are repeated by the clouds in the sky and the leaves of the tree. The antagonistic behavior of the prey and predator has even affected the birds on the right which appear to be quarreling.

With the exception of one branch, which is drawn in red, the entire scene is executed in black line.

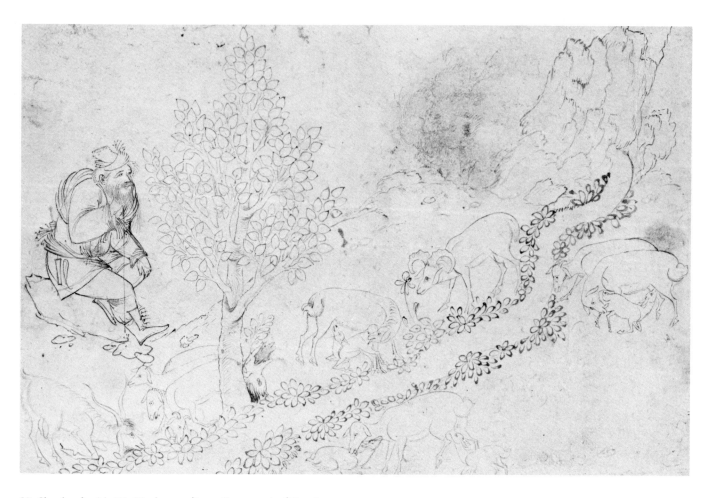

59. Shepherd with His Flock

From the *Riza-i Abbasi Album*
Iran, Safavid period, mid-17th
century

Red line on paper
12.2 x 18.4 cm. (4¹³⁄₁₆ x 7¼ in.)
53.49

The drawing recalls the theme
represented on a previous example
which was executed with polychrome tints (no. 44). This scene,
drawn in red, depicts a shepherd
seated on a rock while his flock
grazes along the banks of a stream
which springs from the mountains
on the upper right and flows
diagonally across the folio. A
dense strip of vegetation grows
along the banks of the stream and
a foliated tree appears on the left.
The animals are rendered with
naturalism, several ewes suckling
or tenderly licking their lambs.
The male members of the flock
are shown with large horns and
include a ram and goat.

The weary shepherd leans on his
staff, enjoying the peace and tranquility of the setting. An impression of external solitude and
harmony permeates the scene, re-
sembling the drawing of the old
man riding a zebu (no. 53).

60. Sketch for *Yusuf va Zulaykha*
From the *Riza-i Abbasi Album*
Iran, Safavid period, mid-17th
   century

Black line on paper
19.8 x 10.4 cm. (7¹³⁄₁₆ x 4⅛ in.)
53.37

The sketch depicts two episodes
from the story of Yusuf and
Zulaykha. On the top is youthful
Yusuf, or Joseph, bound in
chains, kneeling on a carpet with
a flaming halo engulfing his head.
Below him are two other prisoners, also bound in chains attached to a ring placed around
their necks; these two figures have
additional shackles around their
ankles. A candlestick with a burn-
ing candle placed next to Yusuf
indicates the scene takes place in-
doors and at night.

The episode represented on the
lower portion of the drawing occurs several years later and
portrays Yusuf as a middle-aged
man. He is sitting in front of a
gate, holding a sword while his
quiver, bow and shield are placed
in the background. The old
woman approaching him is
Zulaykha who tried so hard to
seduce Yusuf in his earlier days.
Two other women witness this
reunion.

The drawing is perforated and
must have been used to transfer
the design to a manuscript
illustration.

Drawings from India

Drawings executed in India between the 16th and 18th centuries reveal several independent schools in the Deccan and Rajastan in addition to the art of the Mughal court. Mughal painting, influenced by the Safavid traditions during its formative years, soon formed a synthesis of foreign and native elements, creating an indigenous style which had an impact on the development of both Deccani and Rajput schools.

Similar to the tradition in Iran, Mughal drawings are found in the marginal decorations of imperial manuscripts as well as on single sheets incorporated into albums. The most spectacular examples of marginal drawings appear in the albums compiled for Jahangir which combine European themes with local figures and scenes. Due to the fascination with Christianity on the part of the emperors and the colonization of Goa by the Portuguese in the beginning of the 16th century, Western subjects were frequently depicted in the Mughal court.

The Mughal emperors were equally fascinated with historiography; the early rulers, including Babur, Jahangir and Shah Jahan, wrote their own memoirs, while others, like Akbar, commissioned court biographers to document their lives. Many of these biographies were illustrated and as a result of this preoccupation with contemporary history, portraiture became the most popular form of art. Mughal albums contain a great number of portraits, many of which were executed during the lifetime of the subject. The provincial courts followed the traditions of the capital, producing studies of single figures or courtly scenes to be included in albums.

Portraiture was also popular among the Muslim sultans of the Deccan and the Rajput princes of Rajastan and Punjab. The court studios of the Deccan produced album drawings depicting single figures and ceremonial or festive events as well as Christian and Hindu subjects.

The Rajput artists were primarily involved in representing religious themes, particularly the romance of Krishna, the most revered of the Hindu gods.

Mughal School

Islam was introduced to India in the beginning of the eighth century with the conquest of the lower Indus Valley by the Arabs. During the ensuing centuries, several Muslim dynasties controlled various regions of the land, establishing courts in Delhi, Bengal, Kashmir, Gujerat and the Deccan. The Rajput princes of Hindu faith were autonomous in northwestern India, governing in Rajastan and Punjab. These states remained independent until the rise of the Mughal dynasty (1526-1858) which succeeded in uniting the great subcontinent of India under one regime.

Babur (1526-30), the founder of the dynasty, was an outsider like the other Muslim rulers of India and was born in Ferghana, now in Soviet Turkestan. He descended from Timur on his father's side and was related to Genghiz Khan through his mother. In 1504 Babur swept through Afghanistan, capturing Kabul and Ghazna; within the following two decades he was the master of northern India. He defeated the Muslim sultan of Delhi and the Hindu raja of Gwalior in 1526, laying the foundation of the Mughal Empire. The fascinating birth of the new state is narrated in his memoirs, the *Vakiat-i Baburi* which was originally written in Turkish, his native tongue, and later translated into Persian as the *Baburname.*

The newly established dynasty's problems began soon after Babur's death. The reign of Humayun (1530-56), was constantly jeopardized by his ambitious brothers and the Afghans who seized Bengal and forced the emperor into exile. Humayun fled to Iran in 1544 and was welcomed by Shah Tahmasp. The emperor remained in the Safavid court for 10 years, undertaking periodic campaigns to regain his lands with the aid of the Safavids. In 1554 he recaptured Agra and Delhi, defeating his treacherous brothers and the troublesome Afghans.

Humayun's residence in Shah Tahmasp's capital had a considerable impact on the development of Mughal art. The emperor was exposed to the works of the Safavid artists and developed a great admiration for the art of painting. He invited to India two renowned artists from Tabriz, Mir Sayyid Ali and Abd al-Samad, who became highly influential during the formative years of the Mughal school of painting.

During the reign of Akbar (1556-1605), the golden age of India, the empire was reestablished and Mughal art reached its apogee. Akbar was a genius in administrative matters and succeeded in keeping his empire intact by employing Rajput princes in the government. He also married a Hindu princess and formed a strong family bond between the Rajputs and the Mughals. Akbar even advocated a new religion, the Divine Faith, which encompassed all beliefs, and attempted to keep his empire undivided.

The emperor was intellectually inquisitive and extremely liberal, welcoming all talented men to his court. In 1563 he built Fatehpur Sikri, the City of Victory, where Indians of all backgrounds—Jain, Hindu, Muslim, Zoroastrian and Christian—flocked to his court and enjoyed discussions which lasted throughout the night. Akbar had Hindu religious texts, such as the *Mahabharata* and *Ramayana,* translated into Persian, the court language, and compiled a vast library which included manuscripts on all topics.

The emperor had a special liking for illustrated books and established a painting studio comprised of more than 100 artists under the direction of Mir Sayyid and Abd al-Samad.[50] One of the earliest illustrated manuscripts of his reign, the *Tutiname* (Tales of a Parrot), executed around 1560, reveals the eclectic background of the artists with Hindu and Muslim painters from Rajastan, Deccan and Central India working closely together.[51]

Akbar was particularly interested in history and commissioned a number of illustrated historical works, including the monumental *Hamzaname,* the history of Amir Hamza, the uncle of the Prophet Muhammad;[52] and *Baburname* and *Akbarname,* biographies of the two founders of the Mughal Empire.[53] Due to Akbar's fascination with historiography, Mughal painting excelled in the documentation of contemporary events and personages. The most popular theme was portraiture in which the subject was represented with an almost photographic likeness. The court artists also produced albums with single-page paintings and drawings depicting genre scenes, animal studies and portraits (no. 61).

The emperor's reign was not without family problems. His son, Prince Salim, later named Jahangir (Conqueror of the World), was impatient to rule and in 1600 marched to the capital from Allahabad, where he was serving as the governor. Although a showdown was prevented and Akbar forgave the prince, father and son were never fully reconciled.

Jahangir (1605-27), who ascended the throne after the death of his father, continued Akbar's interest in painting but had a completely different taste. He was a true connoisseur and preferred soft and delicate paintings in contrast to the vigorous and dramatic style supported by his father. Jahangir favored single-page paintings which were compiled into

murakkas, or imperial albums. The contents of these albums represent the emperor's taste and interest, showing a predominance of Iranian, Mughal and Deccani paintings as well as European prints which were frequently copied by the court artists.

Two of Jahangir's most celebrated albums are in Tehran and Berlin with a number of detached folios owned by diverse European and American collections. The Tehran volume, known as the *Murakka-i Gulshan* (Gulshan Album) contains 92 folios and is in the Imperial Library of the Gulistan Palace. According to the dated examples, it was compiled between 1599, when Jahangir was still a prince governing Allahabad, and 1609, slightly after his accession.[54] The second volume, owned by the Staatsbibliothek in West Berlin, has 25 folios and is datable between 1608 and 1618.[55]

The albums were compiled in a carefully organized format: each folio contained an illustration on one side and a sample of calligraphy on the other; when the folios were collated, two pages of illustrations faced one another and were followed by two pages of calligraphy; the wide margins around the paintings were decorated with arabesques, whereas those around the text had figural drawings. The figures in these drawings were rendered in color or tints, placed against a landscape executed in gold. Some of the drawings contain the signatures of the best painters of the period, as well as portraits of artists at work and themes copied from European prints.[56] The Freer Gallery of Art owns four folios from the earlier Jahangir album which are included in the exhibition (nos. 62-65).

The painters of Jahangir's studio produced a great number of single-page paintings and drawings which were made for other less sumptuous albums (nos. 66-69). One of the drawings bears an attribution to the most renowned artist of the court, Abu'l-Hasan, who was given the name of Nadir al-Zaman (Wonder of the Age) by Jahangir (no. 68). Abu'l-Hasan was the son of Aka Riza, a well-known painter who worked in the court and executed some of the drawings in the Gulshan album.[57] Abu'l-Hasan was the favorite artist of Jahangir and portrayed his patron in several album paintings.[58] He continued working in the studio after the death of Jahangir and was employed under Shah Jahan. Although other drawings attributed to Abu'l-Hasan are not known, there is no reason to doubt that he also worked in this genre, imitating his father's technique.

Jahangir's son Shah Jahan (1628-58) had spent his early years in Akbar's court and inherited his family's enthusiasm for the

arts. Like his father, he was the son of a Rajput princess and highly devoted to his wife, Mumtaz Mahal, for whom the Taj Mahal was built. Shah Jahan continued to support the activities of the artists and preferred single-page illustrations made for albums (no. 71).

Similar to the fate of his predecessors, Shah Jahan was challenged by his son, Aurangzeb, who had him imprisoned at Agra where he died in 1666. The new ruler, called Alamgir I (1658-1707), undertook campaigns to the south leading to the conquest of the Muslim sultanates of the Deccan in 1686-87. He had the poor judgment to reverse Akbar's attitude towards the Rajputs, arousing their enmity. Alamgir's policies weakened the empire, and soon after his death the Rajput princes as well as the Muslim rulers started fighting against the Mughals.

The Mughal Empire began a slow and painful decline; the state was ruled by weak and incompetent emperors and the outlying provinces gradually slipped away. The imperial studios diminished and the artists sought employment in the provincial courts (no. 72-74). In 1738-39 Nadir Shah, the founder of the Afsharid dynasty of Iran, invaded Delhi and took back the treasures of the emperors (no. 75). The Mughal Empire came to an end in 1858 when the last emperor was exiled to Burma by the British who had extended their power into India.

The traditions established by Akbar, both in administrative and cultural spheres, were so strong that the empire and its arts took a long time to die. The legends of the Mughals are very much alive today, and contemporary paintings still contain vestiges of the past.

61. Babur with Attendants
India, Mughal school, late 16th century

Black line, gold and silver on
   paper; tinted with red, pink,
   blue, green and white
19.1 x 12.2 cm. (7½ x 4¹³⁄₁₆ in.)
54.27

The drawing, which is cropped to
the edge and mounted on heavy
paper, represents a ruler seated on
a canopied platform, attended by
his court. The main personage is
identified as Babur, the founder of
the Mughal Empire, bearing a
close resemblance to the emperor's
representations in the *Baburname*
illustrations. A youthful attendant
stands behind the emperor who
leans against a richly embroidered
cushion while conversing with a
bearded man holding a sheet of
poetry. Seated in front of the platform are a pair of musicians and
several courtiers with attendants.
In the foreground is a pool with a
pair of ducks, surrounded by various types of trees and vegetation;
other trees appear in the background with a large plane tree set
against the rocky mountains.

The secondary elements—the
landscape features, birds, animals
and details of the garments—are
executed in color and gold. The
carpets and cushion around the
emperor are luxuriously decorated
with vibrant colors accentuated by
gold motifs. Silver appears in the
pool and in the two channels con-
nected to it.

The composition recalls the
scheme for outdoor entertainment
scenes which were frequently depicted in the paintings made in
Herat and continued to be produced in the Tabriz studios. The
influence of Safavid painting was
quite strong during Akbar's reign
when the court atelier was under
the direction of the masters from

Tabriz. The same type of setting is also seen in contemporary paintings executed in the Mughal court, particularly in the *Akbar-name* illustrations.

Although the composition is taken from Safavid art, the portrait-like representation of the figures is typically Mughal. The documenation of the lives and activities of the emperors was a major trend in the court with a number of manuscripts devoted to the reigns of Akbar and Babur. Babur had a passion for plants and gardens, which is implied by the setting of the drawing.

62. Five Women in a Landscape
From the *Jahangir Album*
India, Mughal school, ca.
1600-1610

Black line and gold on paper;
    tinted with red, blue, green
    and white
Page: 42.3 x 26.5 cm.
    (16⅝ x 10⁷⁄₁₆ in.)
Text (including borders): 26.3 x
    15.8 cm. (10⅜ x 6¼ in.)
52.2

The verso of the sheet represents a
Mongol chieftain resting in the
countryside, attended by his
courtiers. The side on display contains four panels of *nastalik* calligraphy, two of which are written
on an angle and signed by Ali or
Ali al-Katib. This calligrapher,
who is not very well known, is
mentioned as having come to
India from Meshhed and dying in
Gujerat in 1528-29.[59]

The marginal drawings show the
influence of European prints
which were popular during the
reign of Jahangir and frequently
copied by the court artists. The
five women, placed in a landscape
executed in gold, appear to relate
to Christian themes; however,
since they are taken out of con-
text, it is difficult to determine
their exact iconographical signifi-
cance. The figures are in one way
or another involved with books,
praying before an open volume,
reading or presenting bound
manuscripts.

Their hairstyles and garments are
Western inspired; they wear
belted tunics, long skirts and billowing capes, tinted with varying
tones of golden reds, blues and
greens.

The two women on the top of the
folio flank a table covered with a
red cloth, on which are a pair of
golden rosewater bottles and
candlesticks surrounding an open
book. The female on the right
holds up a painting representing a
haloed saint while her companion
prostrates herself in a praying
position opposite. The figure on
the left margin stands erect, with
an open book in her hand. The
pair below sit on either side of a
cherub-like infant, one extending
a book while the other opens her
arms to receive the crawling
child.

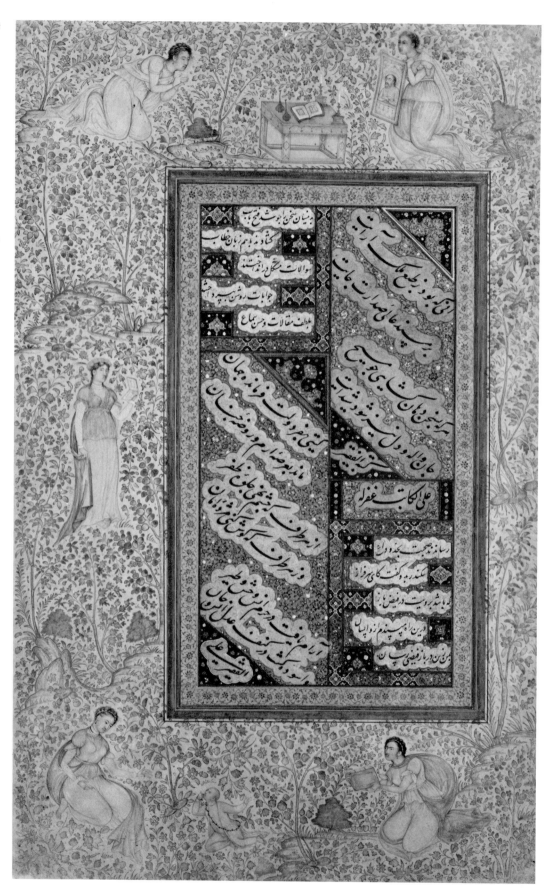

63. Six Artists Preparing Books
From the *Jahangir Album*
India, Mughal school, ca.
1600-1610

Black line and gold on paper;
    tinted with red, pink, blue,
    green and white
Page: 42.5 x 26.6 cm.
    (16¾ x 10½ in.)
Text (including borders): 26.8 x
    15.8 cm. (10⁹⁄₁₆ x 6¼ in.)
54.116

On the verso of this folio is a
painting representing a prince on
horseback who is being handed a
drink from a youth seated on a
tree platform. The recto contains
a sample of calligraphy obliquely
written in *nastalik* and signed by
Mir Ali, a famous 16th-century
calligrapher whose work is frequently included in the Jahangir
albums (nos. 64 and 65). Mir Ali
was from Herat and worked in his
native city until 1528-29 when it
was captured by the Uzbeks who
took him together with several
other artists to their court in
Bukhara. Like his namesake from
Tabriz (nos. 1-7), the calligrapher
excelled in the *nastalik* script and
wrote a great number of samples
for albums until his death in
1558.[60]

The marginal drawings represent
six artists preparing books, each
involved in a different action. The
figures are placed in a landscape
with the hills, trees and flowers
painted in gold against a beige
ground. Their garments and
equipment are highlighted with
polychrome washes which also
have golden tones.

The figure on the upper right is a
papermaker, energetically polish-
ing a sheet with a heavy bur-
nisher. Opposite him is a book-
binder seated in front of a low
table, stamping the cover of a
manuscript; the tools of his trade
are scattered around the table
while several book covers lie on
the ground. Below is another artist who files the edges of a bound
book which is held by a wooden
clamp; a couple of volumes are on
the ground whereas another one,
presumably finished, is placed on

a low chest. The man immediately below is making a wooden bookstand, working with a saw, surrounded by his equipment consisting of various carving tools and blocks. On the lower left, an artist smelts gold, blowing with a long rod the fire lit in an open container; a bar of gold ready to be melted is placed next to him together with several tools and a large golden pot. The last figure represents a calligrapher who is working on a low table; he is writing the text in a bound volume, dipping his brush into a blue-and-white inkwell.

The drawing represents various stages in the production of a book from papermaking to the final step of copying the text. The methods employed by the artists and the specific tools used for different activities are graphically documented, providing an invaluable source for the technology and the arts of the age.

Both the Tehran and Berlin albums contain similar figures in the margins, signed by Aka Riza and Govardhan.[61]

64. European Figures and Scenes
From the *Jahangir Album*
India, Mughal school, ca.
    1600-1610

Black line and gold on paper;
    tinted with red, green and
    yellow
Page: 42.5 x 26.5 cm.
    (16¾ x 10⁷⁄₁₆ in.)
Text (including borders): 26.6 x
    15.6 cm. (10½ x 6⅛ in.)
56.12

A painting depicting a landscape
with chained elephant, attended
by its mahout and a servant, appears on the recto of the folio
while the verso contains three *nastalik* panels. The larger panel is a
quatrain written by Mir Ali, set
against a background adorned
with flowers, blossoming trees
and birds. The same exquisite
decoration appears behind the
smaller panels; the longer strip on
the left also bears the name of Mir
Ali (nos. 63 and 65). Four beauti-
fully drawn birds are placed above
the text.

The figure on the top of the margin portrays the God-Father float-
ing over the universe. The panel
on the upper right, depicting a
female and nude child holding
tablets, is identified by its inscription, "Geometria." The
Christian saint with sheets of
paper who appears below is
thought to be St. Anthony. The
boat on the lower right represents
the Ship of Salvation with the
Christ Child. The group on the
lower left shows the Virgin holding the Christ Child on her right
arm while infant St. John stands
next to her left leg.

The figures are set against a gold
landscape with rocks, trees and
vegetation covering the entire surface; a domed shrine appears behind the ship which sails on a
golden sea.

The marginal drawings are characteristic of the period and represent
an eclectic grouping of 16th-
century religious and mythologi-
cal themes copied from European
prints. Two cartouches below the
ship on the lower right contain
"1580" and "Rome," giving the
date and source of the original
version.

65. Six Men in a Landscape
From the *Jahangir Album*
India, Mughal school, ca.
1600-1610

Black line and gold on paper;
tinted with red, pink, blue,
green and white
Page: 42 x 26.5 cm.
(16½ x 10½ in.)
Text (including borders): 27.5 x
19 cm. (10¹³⁄₁₆ x 7½ in.)
63.4

The verso of the album sheet contains a painting representing Jamshid writing on a rock with a notation that gives the date as 1588 and includes the name of the artist, Abd al-Samad Shirin Kalam. Abd al-Samad, invited to the Mughal court by Humayun in 1556, was put in charge of the imperial painting studios during Akbar's reign and continued working in the capital until the turn of the century.

The marginal decoration of the recto contains considerably more color and represents six figures in a landscape with birds and insects hovering around the trees and flowers. The *nastalik* texts in the center of the folio are adorned with similar motifs, executed in color. The obliquely written panel is signed by Mir Ali whose works were included in two other folios (nos. 63 and 64).

The figures in the margins appear to be occupied with astrological calculations and represent courtly types. On the upper left is a young prince attired in a translucent white robe, standing on a stool and praying with his arms extended. The older figure behind him repeats the gesture while a half-naked ascetic, sitting on the far left, observes the pair. Below him is a courtly figure, who sits on a chair and reads a book. On the lower portion of the margin an astrologer holds up an astrolabe; an open book, a roll of paper and writing utensils are placed on the sheet spread in front. The astrologer is most likely calculating the horoscope of the figure seated opposite, who is attired in fashionable garments of the court and bears a sword.

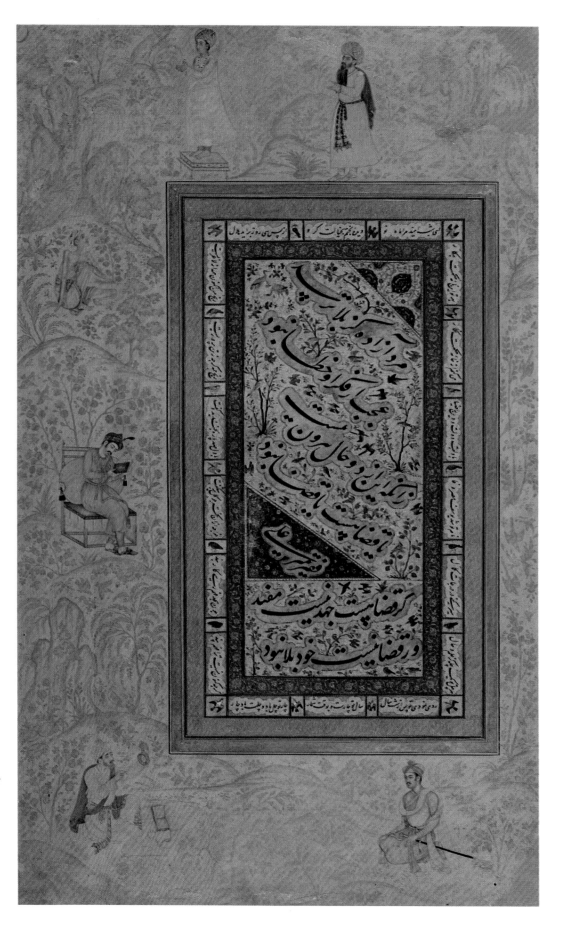

This folio was prepared with extreme care, combining the best talents of Jahangir's court as observed in the delicate execution of the figures and landscape decorating the margins, the beautiful illumination with flowers and birds harmoniously balanced by the fine script.

66. Pilgrim with an Ascetic
India, Mughal school, early 17th century

Black line on paper; tinted with red, blue and green
Page: 25 x 15.8 cm.
  (9⅞ x 6¼ in.)
Drawing: 10.4 x 9.3 cm.
  (4⅛ x 3¾ in.)
29.76

This example depicts a landscape with two figures, one of whom is a half-naked ascetic. The drawing, also mounted on cardboard with a marginal decoration placed around it, was adjusted to fit the opening by the addition of two panels of marbled paper above and below, using several carelessly executed borders to camouflage the seams. The marginal decorations, executed in gold, are pasted sideways and depict a pair of roosters and deer in a landscape.

The drawing represents a pilgrim holding an open book, discussing its contents with the ascetic who is realistically portrayed as a wiry, emaciated man. Their seemingly contradictory lives which achieve the same spiritual end is symbolized by the two trees in the center with a flowering shrub intertwined around a cypress tree.

The landscape and portions of the protagonists' garments are tinted in color while the faces are executed in soft brush strokes.

67. Sultan Parviz with an Ascetic
India, Mughal school, early 17th century

Black line, gold and silver on
 paper; tinted with red, pink,
 green, yellow and white
Page: 30 x 18.8 cm.
 (11¹³⁄₁₆ x 7⅜ in.)
Drawing: 15 x 8.6 cm.
 (5⅞ x 2⅝ in.)
29.3

The tinted drawing is pasted on a
sheet which depicts a landscape
with figures and is backed with
cardboard. Strips of gold and
silver are carelessly placed around
the drawing, attempting to frame
the scene and to fit it into the
blank area between the marginal
decorations.

The scene in the margin, executed
in gold and silver on a pink
ground, represents a brook which
flows around and under the drawing, its banks covered with blossoming trees and clusters of flowers. On the right an ascetic, wearing only a stole and a loincloth,
converses with a man holding a
book. The sheet is older than the
drawing as the latter was adjusted
to fit into the allotted space with
an extra strip added to the top.
The marginal decoration is beauti-
fully executed although the oxida-
tion of the silver has somewhat
lessened its rich coloring.

According to the inscription, the
tinted drawing represents Sultan
Parviz who was one of the sons of
Jahangir. The young prince is attired in the characteristic garments of the age: he wears a flat
turban, a tight bodice and pants
and long skirt tied with flowing
embroidered sash; a string of
pearls and a jeweled necklace hang
around his neck while a dagger is
tucked into his belt. He converses
with a holy man who holds a ro-
sary in one hand, a pouch and a
stick in the other; the ascetic is
naked except for his loincloth and
long hair which falls in streaming
locks to his waist. The figures are
standing by a stream, below a
large plane tree partially cut by
the frame. Soft washes appear in
the garments and landscape with
touches of gold accentuating the
jewelry of the prince.

This example was executed during
the reign of Jahangir and it appears
that a suitable margin was sought
to enhance the drawing.

68. Youth with a Book

Attributed to Nadir al-Zaman
India, Mughal school, early 17th
century

Black line and gold on paper;
  tinted with red, pink, blue
  and yellow
Page: 15 x 10 cm.
  (5⅞ x 3¹⁵⁄₁₆ in.)
Drawing: 12.5 x 7.3 cm.
  (4⅞ x 2⅞ in.)
07.161

The drawing presents a sensitive
portrait of a young man engrossed
in his book; it is mounted on
cardboard and framed with a
border of gold leaves on a scrolling blue vine. The inscription,
added almost a century and a half
later, states that this is the work
of Nadir al-Zaman, the court
painter of Emperor Jahangir, and
gives the year 1768. The attribution could very well be valid as
the fine execution of line and
elaborate working of the details
can be found in the other works of
Abu'l-Hasan, who was given the
name Nadir al-Zaman by his patron, Jahangir.

The portrait is possibly one of the
earliest works of the artist who
was trained by his father, Aka
Riza, also employed in Jahangir's
court studio. The artistic conven-
tion of depicting courtly figures
with one leg crossed over the
other and the hand holding a
handkerchief resting on the knee
was established in the Safavid
court and continued to be employed by the Mughal artists. The
high stool, one shoe lying on the
ground and the slightly bent head
are conventions also found in
Safavid paintings (no. 23).

Gold is used in the metallic
portions of the garments, such as
the embroidery on the turban,
belt and handkerchief as well as in
the stamped cover of the book and
in the scabbard of the sword. Red
is employed to accentuate parts of
the outfit and to suggest the precious gems on the scabbard. Faint
washes of pink, blue and yellow
appear on the turban, undershirt
and book, providing a soft and
delicate coloring in keeping with
the youthfulness of the subject.

69. Landscape with Animals
India, Mughal school, early 17th
  century

Black line on paper
25.7 x 15.4 cm. (10⅛ x 6⅟₁₆ in.)
07.618

This example—badly damaged,
stained and repaired—was possibly a sample page for animal and
plant studies. The animals are
scattered around the sheet which
represents several vignettes inter-
mingled with fine drawings of
flowering plants. In the lower
portion are a pair of cranes, a goat
trying to feed on the leaves of a
tree on which a peacock is perched
and a doe attending her young.
Above are birds resting on a fruit
tree, flowers, other birds and a
leopard stalking a pair of mountain goats. On the top of the folio
is a lion killing a stag while the
mate runs away.

These studies were later incorporated into manuscripts, used
either in the paintings, marginal
decorations or on lacquer bookbindings. They also served as
models for carpets, textiles and
other arts which relied on the designs determined by the court
artists.

70. Animal Kingdom
India, Mughal school, early 17th
  century

Black line on paper; tinted with
  pink, blue, green and yellow
Page: 34.1 x 21.9 cm.
  (13⅜ x 8⅝ in.)
Drawing: 23.4 x 11.8 cm.
  (9³⁄₁₆ x 4⅝ in.)
45.29

This exquisite drawing represents
the peaceable animal kingdom
with a profusion of creatures skill-
fully blended into the composition, each depicted in its most
characteristic pose. Mughal artists
excelled in studies of animals and,
with the exception of portraiture,
this genre truly represents their
acute observation and refined talents. There are close to 100 birds
and beasts depicted in this small
drawing, and yet each animal appears as an individual study.

The drawing is mounted on heavy
paper; it has several gold, black
and blue lines enclosing a band of
gold floral designs on a pink
ground, cut into strips to form a
border. The marginal decoration,
depicting cranes and ducks in a
landscape, is executed in black
and gold lines on cream paper,
matching the theme of the central
drawing.

The drawing, tinted in the palest tones, represents the animals as they appear in nature with the creatures of the sky on the top, the inhabitants of land in the center and those who dwell in the seas at the bottom. The animals are shown within their natural habitat with the fish, crocodile, crabs and seals in the water; the reptiles, snakes and a fantastic dragon appear on the shore. The land animals include elephants, tigers, lions, pheasants, foxes, horses, rhinoceroses, camels, deer, goats, sheep, monkeys, bears and cats which gradually lead the eye up the folio, toward the tree in the background.[62] Diverse birds perch on the tree and rocks or fly into the scene; included among them are ducks, sparrows and a superb phoenix. The artist has combined both domestic and wild creatures, as well as real and imaginary creatures, in a single scene.

This drawing, similar to the examples discussed previously (nos. 66-69), does not belong to the famous imperial collections of Jahangir. However, it reveals the high technical and aesthetic developments of the painters whose works were compiled into less sumptuous but equally exciting albums.

71. Hunting Scene
India, Mughal school, mid-17th
   century

Black line, gold and silver on
   paper; tinted with red
   and green
Page: 25.7 x 18 cm.
   (10⅛ x 7¹⁄₁₆ in.)
Drawing: 16.4 x 14.3 cm.
   (6⁷⁄₁₆ x 5⅝ in.)
07.204

The drawing, which includes its
original gold frame, is mounted
on cardboard with additional
borders added at a later date. The
silver applied to the background
has oxidized, leaving unattractive
dark stains; the portion of water
in the foreground was cut out at a
later period and replaced by a
silver strip, which has also
oxidized.

The scene depicts a princely hunt
with a young rider shooting arrows at a powerful lion which
reels back from the impact. Foxes
and hares, frightened by the attack, scamper in either direction;
the attendant of the hunter, his
turban unwound in the excite-
ment, tries to run out of the way.

A palatial structure appears
amidst the mountains and trees in
the background with two workers
strolling toward it. The serenity
of the setting, accentuated by a
pair of foxes peacefully resting on
the rocks, contrasts with the vio-
lent drama of the hunt unfolding
in the foreground.

An impression of depth is created
by the progression of planes and
the diminishing size of elements,
employing perspective in a most
successful manner. Faint washes of
red and green are used in the
landscape while gold highlights
the weapons of the hunter and the
trappings of his mount.

72. Woman Carrying a Basket
India, Mughal school, early 18th century

Black line and gold on paper; tinted with red
Page: 37 x 23.3 cm.
   (14⅝ x 9⅛ in.)
Drawing: 13.2 x 23.3 cm.
   (5³⁄₁₆ x 2⁷⁄₁₆ in.)
07.211

This example represents the provincial Mughal style which appeared after the empire began to lose its authority and could not support the artists, forcing them to seek employment in the provinces. It depicts a young woman carrying a large basket on her head and attired in traditional Mughal garments with a long flowing scarf, short-sleeved bodice and long skirt. Gold accentuates the brocaded portions of her outfit (such as the edges of the scarf and bodice and the horizontal bands in the skirt) and represents her jewelry (the armlets, bracelets and necklace) as well as her gilded shoes. Touches of red appear in the skirt and shoes and highlight the inlaid gems of her jewelry.

The drawing has been mounted on a blank sheet with green and gold marbled paper pasted around it. The marbled paper has been sprayed with gold which has spilled onto the drawing.

73. Two Women with Attendants

India, Mughal school, mid-18th
century

Black line, gold and silver on
paper; tinted with red, blue,
green and white
Page: 40.6 x 29.3 cm.
(16 x 11⁹⁄₁₆ in.)
Drawing: 23.2 x 17.8 cm.
(9⅛ x 7 in.)
07.213

The drawing portrays two young
ladies seated on a terrace overlook-
ing a body of water beyond which
is a strip of land with a large
complex. The ladies are attended
by two servants who hold
peacock-tail fans and are enter-
tained by a quartet of musicians
and singers who clap their hands.
Joining their group are three
other women and an attendant
who is preparing potent and aro-
matic concoctions from the contents of bottles and jars spread in
front of her.

The drawing, pasted on blank
paper, is enclosed by a gold-
speckled red sheet and has a blue
border decorated with gold floral
motifs. The landscape elements
are fully colored with green trees
filling the background; the pond,
barely visible behind the trees,
was originally painted silver and
now is oxidized. Certain features,
such as the two fountains—one on
the terrace where the ladies sit
and the other behind them—are
unfinished with only the outlines
of the streams of water sketched
in.

The two ladies sit on a carpet,
leaning against large cushions;
they are smoking water pipes
while discussing the contents of a
book. Placed on the carpet are
other volumes; between the figures is a group of cups and bowls
on a mat which is barely
sketched.

The setting most likely depicts
one of the provincial Mughal
courts with a large fortified palace
and its suburbs represented on the
shore beyond the water.

74. Woman with Attendants
India, Mughal school, early 18th
 century

Black line and gold on paper;
 tinted with red and white
Page: 21.5 x 14.9 cm.
 (8⁷⁄₁₆ x 5⅞ in.)
Drawing: 15.5 x 9.2 cm.
 (6⅛ x 3⅜ in.)
07.607

This drawing depicts a lady seated
in the courtyard of a palace, accompanied by five attendants. It
is mounted on an album sheet
with a 14-line text on the back;
the margins around the drawing
are painted blue and speckled
with gold.

A group of three women appears
in the foreground; one reclines
against a cushion, another listens
to music while the third plays a
tambourine. Above them is the
main personage, flanked by two
attendants, one of whom offers
her a drink in a small cup. Long-
necked bottles, bowls of fruit,
covered boxes and trays with
small footed bowls containing delicacies are scattered around the
courtyard. A domed pavilion with
carved panels depicting bowls and
bottles rises in the background
with a group of trees seen above
the walls of the enclosure.

Gold is used to accentuate the details of the garments and jewelry;
it is also applied to the metal vessels. Red appears on the hands
and feet of the women, suggesting
that they were painted with
henna; white is used to represent
the pearl jewelry. Two of the
women, on the upper left and
lower right, have lighter complex-
ions, their skins painted in soft
washes of white.

The theme of idle women amus-
ing themselves within the confines of their palaces seems to have
been quite popular in the provincial courts, attempting to recreate
the luxurious environment of the
Mughal capital.

75. Portrait of Nadir Shah
India, Mughal school, mid-18th
  century

Black line on paper; tinted with
  red, mauve, green, yellow,
  brown and white
Page: 37.9 x 23.9
  ($14^{15}/_{16}$ x $9^{7}/_{16}$ in.)
Drawing: 19.7 x 10.4 cm.
  ($7^{3}/_{4}$ x $4^{1}/_{16}$ in.)
07.256

The portrait, mounted on a blank
cardboard, is decorated with
coarsely executed marbled paper
which has been added around the
drawing at a later date. The original sheet has been slightly
trimmed and now is framed by
gold, red and green lines.

The portrait is executed in black
with only the face, headdress and
fur collar depicted in color. The
figure is shown in profile, seated
against a thick cushion holding a
sword across his knees. An inscription identifying the subject
appears below and states that it is
the representation of Nadir Shah.

The unusual headdress, possibly
Nadir Shah's personal choice for
the Afsharid rulers, is a tall yellow cap embroidered with green
leaves and red blossoms; a pearl
garland decorates the crown which
is softly gathered at the top and
mounted with a feather attached
by a ruby pin; the upturned
split-rim is painted mauve.

Nadir Shah is represented with an
unfaltering stern expression, true
to the reputation of this remarkable man who saved Iran from foreign domination, expanded its
boundaries and invaded India in
1738-39. The strong profile of
the subject is accentuated by the
soft-brown fur collar of his coat
and pale-green shirt. This is most
likely a contemporary portrait
executed shortly after Nadir
Shah's Indian campaign.

Nadir Shah, born in 1688, belonged to the Turkmen tribe of the Afshars. He entered the services of Shah Tahmasp II and fought valiantly against the Afghans in the east and the Ottomans in the west, defending the remnants of the Safavid state. After being proclaimed king of Iran in 1736, he immediately set out to capture Kandahar and then marched onto Delhi. In the decisive battle of 1739, Nadir Shah was the victor. He reinstated the Mughal emperor, Muhammed Shah, in return for the provinces north of the Indus plus a phenomenal sum of money and treasures, including the renowned Koh-i Nur diamond and the fabled Peacock Throne. The amount levied was so large that the Iranians were exempted from taxes for three years. Nadir Shah was assassinated in 1747 in an uprising instigated by a group of Afshar and Kajar chiefs.

Deccani School

The sultans of the Deccan, the high plateau in the southern portion of India, were late arrivals like the Mughals. Among the first Muslims to rule this region were the Bahmanids (1347-1527) whose capital at Bidar became a major center of learning. The Bahmanids set up diplomatic and cultural exchanges with the Ottomans, employing Turks, Persians and Arabs in their courts.

When the effective rule of the Bahmanids disintegrated at the end of the 15th century, a major portion of the Deccan became divided between five dynasties. The Barid-Shahis, who replaced the Bahmanids in Bidar, fell to the Adil-Shahis of Bijapur in 1619; the Imad-Shahis of Berar (1485-1572) were eventually absorbed by the Nizam-Shahis; the Adil-Shahis of Bijapur (1490-1686), who were related to the Ottoman sultans, were particularly interested in the development of the arts and invited scholars and painters from Turkey and Iran to their courts; the Nizam-Shahis (1491-1633) ruled in Ahmednagar and vicinity; and the Kutb-Shahis (1512-1686), who controlled Golconda, were the descendants of the Karakoyunlu Turkmens.

Despite the continuous rivalries and endless wars among these states, Deccani painting flourished between the middle of the 16th century until the Mughal conquest of 1686-87, the most prolific studios being in Bijapur, Ahmednagar and Golconda. The artists created remarkable works which reveal a mixture of local traditions, Ottoman, Safavid and Mughal court styles, and to some extent the influence of Western painting. Portraiture was a predominant genre although occasional *Ragamala* series and Christian themes were also produced (nos. 76-77).

76. Woman Holding a Vina
India, Deccani school, ca. 1670

Black line on paper
16.6 x 11.3 cm. (6⁹⁄₁₆ x 4⁷⁄₁₆ in.)
46.27

The drawing, which has been stained and repaired around the edges, represents a seated woman holding a vina, the traditional string instrument of India. She has stopped playing momentarily and smells a flower while watching the cautiously approaching deer which has been attracted by the music.

Clusters of flowers cover the ground, and three different types of trees grow in the background. The largest, framing the seated woman, has blossom-like leaves; several birds appear amidst the leaves while two squirrels run up the trunk. A castle rises behind the hills on the upper right.

The composition indicates that the scene illustrates the Todi Ragini from a *Ragamala* series. The *Ragamala,* literally translated as a Garland of Musical Modes, is a codification of Hindu music which is expressed with verses and pictorial representation. It symbolizes the aesthetics of Hindu music and contains a great number of variations although traditionally there are six fundamental *ragas,* or "melody moulds," each of which contains five *raginis,* or modes. The Todi Ragini is represented by a woman playing the vina, attracting deer.

The drawing, rendered only in soft black lines, is extremely refined with delicate strokes defining the figure, animals and landscape elements. The artist has successfully captured the sentiment expressed by the musical mode, representing a pictorial version of the theme.

77. Virgin and Child
India, Deccani school, ca. 1625

Black line and gold on paper;
  tinted with red, pink and white
Page: 36 x 23 cm.
  (14¾₁₆ x 9¹⁄₁₆ in.)
Drawing: 16 x 11.1 cm.
  (6⁵⁄₁₆ x 4⅜ in.)
07.155

The tinted drawing representing
the Virgin and Child has been
mounted on blank cardboard with
several red and blue borders used
to frame the scene. The Virgin
Mary is shown seated beneath a
tree with the Christ Child who
holds up a book. They are surrounded by bunches of leaves and
flowers and richly foliated trees
with streams of branches drooping
down the soft hills.

The execution of the figures is
highly stylized with crisply drawn
drapery forming decorative folds.
The Virgin wears a long flowing
scarf tinted pink; her dress is
lined in red and slightly open at
front, revealing a white undershirt; elaborate gold jewelry
adorns her neck and ears. The figures were obviously inspired by
European examples but executed
in a local style and technique.
Their facial types also suggest a
native tradition.

The soft brush strokes in the landscape with delicately drawn leaves
and branches contrast with the
rigidity of line seen in the figures.
Obviously the artist was more at
ease executing the background
and labored over the figures.

Deccani artists were quite familiar
with Christian themes; since the
Portuguese had established a col-
ony in Goa in 1510, Jesuit mis-
sionaries and European travelers
were constant visitors. This drawing is attributed to the school of
Bijapur which was in close contact
with Portuguese settlements.

129

Rajput School

The Rajputs, the Hindu rulers of India, were renowned for their brave and chivalrous conduct as well as for their strong tribal ties which prevented them from uniting against the foreign invaders. The Rajput princes established a number of states in Rajastan and the Punjab Hills which paid tribute to the Mughals at the height of their empire, between the early 17th and the mid-18th century. After the slackening of Mughal authority, the Rajputs became more or less autonomous until the arrival of the British in the early part of the 19th century.

Rajput painting in the Punjab Hills developed after the 17th century, most likely stimulated by the close contact with the Mughal court. The painting studios flourished during the following two centuries and produced remarkable portraits and series of religious paintings with an overwhelming preference for the Krishna cycle.[63] The court painters of Kangra were particularly active during the second half of the 18th century and developed an indigenous style which reached its height under the patronage of Sansar Chand (1775-1823).[64] The raja and the members of his family commissioned a great number of portraits, single-page paintings and voluminous series narrating the life and teaching of Krishna and his romance with Radha.

One fascinating series was devoted to the mystical romance of Princess Damayanti who falls in love with Nala, the young king of Nishadha, originally written around the middle of the 12th century by Sriharsha. The poem relates the meeting of the two protagonists, their wedding, misfortunes and ultimate happiness, stressing the lifelong devotion of the lovers whom the gods had destined should be together.

The story was particularly significant to Sansar Chand, who fought valiantly against the Afghan invasion and ruled supreme in the Kangra Valley for two decades; he himself had a passionate love affair with the beautiful Nokhu whom he abducted and later married. The hero and heroine of the *Romance of Nala and Damayanti* were probably associated with the patron and his wife and the setting of the story inspired by the raja's palaces.

Several sets of the *Romance of Nala and Damayanti* were executed between 1790 and 1810, each set conceived as a series of some 100 paintings. Some of these sets were completed while others contain only portions of the story; the illustrations in a couple of the sets are merely sketched and left unfinished.

One of the incomplete and unfinished sets was made around 1790 or 1800 and contains about 47 illustrations owned by various American collections, including the Freer Gallery of Art (nos. 78-82).[65] The scenes illustrate the second part of the *Romance of Nala and Damayanti* and are executed in a technique which is particular to this series. The illustrations are sketched in sanguine, or a broad red line, over which a second black line was drawn; a semitransparent white ground was applied over these lines, covering the entire sheet, serving as a primer and facilitating corrections; then fine brush strokes completed the drawing which was now ready for the final coloring rendered in gouache, or opaque watercolor; color was first applied to the background and then to the figures.

The illustrations are on rectangular sheets of paper approximately 29.2 by 40 centimeters (11½ by 15¾ inches) with a border of 3.5 centimeters (1⅜ inches) left blank on four sides; the dimensions of the drawings average 22.2 by 33.5 centimeters (8⅝ by 13³⁄₁₆ inches). This format and size are common to all the existing sets.

The Freer sketches are executed in fine black lines on a white ground with only the preliminary tints applied to the background. The figures are rendered with great charm, gliding through the scenes with serenity and grace. Although a firm outline is used, there is an ease of motion with the elements flowing into one another. The Nala-Damayanti scenes represent the grand style of the Rajput school in the Kangra Valley.

78. Toilet of Damayanti
From the *Romance of Nala and Damayanti*
India, Rajput school, ca. 1790-1800

Black line over white ground on paper; tinted with red, mauve, green and yellow
Page: 29.2 x 40 cm.
  (11½ x 15¾ in.)
Drawing: 22.3 x 33.7 cm.
  (8¾ x 13¼ in.)
30.85

The depiction of several consecutive episodes in the drawing is characteristic of the Nala-Damayanti illustrations. The scene takes place in Damayanti's palace prior to her marriage; it shows the princess being washed and groomed and departing for the wedding pavilion. The beautiful Damayanti, half nude with her long black hair loose, is seated on a stool in the center of the courtyard; some of her maidens bathe her while others hold up a curtain for privacy.

Two of the maidens hold ewers, one pouring a ewer's contents over Damayanti's head; another pair fills the containers from large jars while two others hold a towel and a mirror. Placed on the ground in front of Damayanti are various bathing utensils such as jars, basins and bowls.

The next vignette depicts Damayanti being groomed and admired by her maidens in the pavilion which appears on the upper left. The attendants cluster around her: some paint her toenails and fingernails; others hold up a mirror, carry cosmetics on trays, select jewelry from a chest and shield her with a scarf; an elderly woman carries an incense burner. Two musicians outside play the vina and drum; an attendant walks by with a covered tray.

In the kitchen on the upper right, the cooks are preparing for the wedding feast, cooking rice in a large kettle, kneading dough and bringing in supplies. The wedding pavilion appears behind the screen in the background, its open roof decorated with birds.

The departure of Damayanti is depicted on the lower right. A maiden appears at the door, handing to the priest an ewer to be used during the ceremonies. Damayanti, her head bowed in modesty, is attended by several friends on her way to the wedding pavilion.

Black lines have been used to go over or to correct the original sketch, which is barely visible under the semitransparent white ground. The preliminary washes have been applied to certain portions of the scene, such as the courtyard, curtains, a few vessels and Damayanti's robe.

79. Marriage of Damayanti

From the *Romance of Nala and Damayanti*

India, Rajput school, ca. 1790-1800

Black line over white ground on paper; tinted with red, mauve, green and yellow

22.1 x 16.3 cm. (8^{11}/₁₆ x 6⅜ in.)

23.11

The illustration, damaged and trimmed along the edges, has been cut in half and includes only the left portion of the scene. The drawing represents the wedding ceremonies of Nala and Damayanti, who are seated in the marriage pavilion which was seen in the previous episode. In front of the couple is the priest Gautama who ties their hands with a cord, symbolizing the marriage knot. The elderly figure bearing a crown next to the priest is King Bhima, the bride's father. He brings to his new son-in-law several gifts, including the miraculous sword of Durga, a dagger and a covered box on a tray which most likely contains the wish-fulfilling wreath of gems originally given to him by Siva.

The maidens around the central figures carry garlands, trays, bottles and flaming torches. The woman bending over the bride is probably Kala, Damayanti's faithful companion. Spread in front of the bridal couple are various ceremonial vessels, such as bowls, basins and vases.

In the foreground, outside the enclosure, are attendants and torch-bearers who accompany an elephant laden with baggage and a chariot drawn by a pair of horses, also given to Nala by King Bhima.

This illustration has also been corrected and the original lines under the semitransparent white ground are still visible; preliminary colors have been added to the background.

80. Departure for Nisadha

From the *Romance of Nala and Damayanti*

India, Rajput school, ca. 1790-1800

Black line over white ground on paper; tinted with red, mauve, green, yellow and white

Page: 29.2 x 40 cm. (11½ x 15¾ in.)

Drawing: 22.2 x 33.5 cm. (8¾ x 13³⁄₁₆ in.)

23.10

This episode takes place after the wedding of the hero and heroine and represents Damayanti departing from her father's house to go with her husband to his kingdom of Nisadha. Damayanti, riding in her palanquin, is leaving the courtyard accompanied by King Bhima and Prince Dama, both of whom bear crowns. Also joining the retinue are scores of Damayanti's maidens, some holding fly whisks and the others mourning her departure. A group of musicians heads the procession, which moves through the screen rolled back by the attendants and leaves through the palace gate.

Nala is seated in the balcony on the upper left, conversing with a man while being fanned with a fly whisk. Other maidens watch the procession from the cantilevered` windows of the palace.

The narration of the departure continues in the fields outside the palace. Nala, sitting in the chariot given by his father-in-law, is moving along with his entourage and baggage, preceded by flagbearers and musicians. Beyond the hill is Damayanti's palanquin and her train, which includes servants bearing large boxes on their heads or carrying huge caskets by poles, her mounted attendants and elephants, as well as her wedding bed and throne.

The highly crowded scene contains more preliminary colors than the previous drawings with the sky, hills and details of the baggage executed in pale tones.

81. Damayanti with the Lotus

From the *Romance of Nala and Damayanti*
India, Rajput school, ca. 1790-1800

Black line and silver over white ground on paper; tinted with mauve, blue, green, yellow and beige
Page: 29.2 x 39.8 cm.
(11½ x 15¹¹⁄₁₆ in.)
Drawing: 22.2 x 33.4 cm.
(8¾ x 13⅛ in.)
23.13

After Nala and Damayanti settle in Nisadha, they spend their days in blissful happiness, proving their unwavering devotion to each other. The scenes representing the great love that exists between the lovers are set within the tranquility of their palace, its serene atmosphere enhanced by the elegant figures and their lyric postures.

In this episode Nala is jesting with Damayanti and Kala. He has given Damayanti a lotus which she considers more valuable than anything else in the world since it was from her beloved. The couple are seated in an arcaded pavilion in front of which is a fountain with three ducks walking around. Several maidens stroll in the courtyard, conversing or carrying trays into the two structures on either side. Rows of trees border the fountain and appear behind the high walls of the enclosure.

In the center of the scene are Nala and Damayanti, seated on a couch. Nala rests his arms on the two cushions on his lap while conversing with Damayanti who bends her head in modesty, holding the lotus in her hand as Kala stands beside her. Scattered around the floor are a low table with small bottles, a spittoon for betels, a jar and a covered bowl.

The setting was likely inspired by the palaces of Sansar Chand, the patron of the work, and represents the luxurious structures of the Kangra Valley. These palaces with high walls—enclosing a complex of arcaded pavilions placed around the courtyards adorned with gardens, fountains and pools—reflect the architectural traditions established by the Mughals in the 16th and 17th centuries.

82. Lovers Watching Sunset

From the *Romance of Nala and Damayanti*
India, Rajput school, ca. 1790-1800

Black line and silver over white ground on paper; tinted with red, pink, green, yellow and black
Page: 29.2 x 39.8 cm.
  (11½ x 15¹¹⁄₁₆ in.)
Drawing: 22.2 x 33.4 cm.
  (8¾ x 13⅛ in.)
23.12

One of the most charming scenes in the *Romance of Nala and Damayanti* represents the lovers watching the sunset from their palace; Damayanti is mourning the fate of the *cakravaka* birds which separate from one another before darkness sets in. The couple is seated in an arcaded wing, leaning against a large pillow; they point to the birds which walk around the rocky shore across the water. Cushions, trays and bowls lie on the ground beside the figures.

Outside the pavilion are two maidens seated at the edge of a pool, dipping their feet into the water. Three other women appear in the doorway and arcades of the structure.

The background of the scene—sky, trees and hills—is painted in pale tones; touches of color also appear in the skin of the women, while the water is rendered in silver.

The sentiment expressed by Damayanti—mourning the separation of lovers—symbolizes the theme of eternal love and devotion which permeates the poem.

Notes

1. The manuscripts was first published in F. R. Martin, *Miniatures from the Period of Timur in a Ms. of the Poems of Sultan Ahmad Jalair*, Vienna, 1926. In this publication Martin describes how he obtained the work in Istanbul. A thorough study of the *Divan*, its painter and date appears in Deborah E. Klimburg-Salter, "A Sufi Theme in Persian Painting: the *Divan* of Sultan Ahmad Galair in the Freer Gallery of Art, Washington, D.C.," *Kunst des Orients*, vol. XI, nos. 1-2 (1976-77), pp. 43-84.

2. Istanbul, Topkapi Palace Museum, II. 2153 and H. 2160. Another almost contemporary album is in Berlin, Staatsbibliothek, Diez A Fol. 70-73. The latter, with full references to the two Istanbul albums, is published in M. Ş. Ipşiroğlu, *Saray-Alben*, Wiebaden, 1964.

3. M. Ş. Ipşiroğlu, *Siyah Qalem*, Graz, 1976.

4. Tabriz was occupied by the Kipchaks in 1385, by the Timurids in 1386 and by the Karakoyunlus in 1387 and 1406; Baghdad was taken by Timur in 1393 and 1401 and by the Karakoyunlus in 1403.

5. Illustrated manuscripts executed in the court of Sultan Ahmed are:
(a) *Khamsa* of Nizami (London, British Library, Or. 13297)
  1386 and 1388, Baghdad, copied by Mahmud ibn Muhammed
(b) *Ajaib al-Makhlukat* of al-Kazvini (Paris, Bibliothèque Nationale, suppl. pers. 332)
  1392, Baghdad (?), copied by Ahmed of Herat
(c) *Kalila va Dimna* (Paris, Bibliothèque Nationale, suppl. pers. 913)
  1392, Baghdad (?), copied by al-Hafiz Ibrahim
(d) *Three Poems* of Khvaju Kirmani (London, British Library, Add. 18113)
  1396, Baghdad, copied by Mir Ali of Tabriz, painted by Junayd
(e) *Kitab al-Bulhan* (Oxford, Bodleian Library, Or. 133)
  Written in Arabic
  1399, Baghdad (?), copied and painted by Abd al-Hasan ibn Ali ibn al-Hasan of Baghdad
(f) *Divan* of Sultan Ahmad (Washington, D.C., Freer Gallery of Art, 32.29-32.37)
  ca. 1400, Baghdad (?), copied by (att.): Mir Ali of Tabriz
(g) *Khosrau va Shirin* of Nizami (Washington, D.C., Freer Gallery of Art, 31.29-31.37)
  Before 1410, Tabriz, copied by Ali ibn Hasan al-Sultani
See Also Dorothea Duda, "Die Buchmalerei der Galairden," part I, *Der Islam*, vol. 48 (1971), pp. 28-192; part II, *ibid.*, vol. 49 (1972), pp. 153-220

6. When the *Divan* entered the Freer Gallery, the folios with the drawings were removed from the manuscripts before it was paginated. In Martin's publication, it is mentioned that the illustrations began on folio 17. Following the sequence of the reproductions in Martin's book, the accession numbers of the Freer Gallery and the text, we were able to determine the order and location of the drawings within the manuscript.

7. London, British Library, Add. 18113 (Charles Rieu, *Catalogue of the Persian Manuscripts in the British Museum*, London, 1966, vol. II, pp. 620-622; Norah M. Titley, *Miniatures from Persian Manuscripts*, London, 1977, no. 251).

8. Abd al-Hayy was trained by Shams al-Din and taught the sultan to paint. After Timur conquered Baghdad, he took Abd al-Hayy together with other Jalairid artists to his court in Samarkand where the painter died. Abd al-Hayy is said to have become extremely religious toward the end of his life and destroyed his paintings. Several paintings and drawings, either signed by him or copied by a later Timurid artist named Muhammed al-Hayyam, appear in the Istanbul and Berlin albums (Klimburg-Salter, "A Sufi Theme"). Timur is also said to have taken Mir Ali of Tabriz to Samarkand (Rieu, *Catalogue of Persian Manuscripts*, p. 622).

9. Folios 311b, 312a, 323b, 328b, 329a and 336a. On two of these folios, a line or two of poetry appears on the top or bottom, although there are no marginal lines (fols. 311b and 336a). There are also several other folios which are one-third empty (fols. 282b, 317a and 328a). Another completely empty folio without the original marginal lines is now entirely filled with the works of Sadi (fol. 282a).

10. Edwin Binney, 3rd, *Turkish Miniature Paintings and Manuscripts from the Collection of Edwin Binney, 3rd*, New York and Los Angeles, 1973, no. 29.

11. Ipşiroğlu, *Siyah Qalem*, pl. 55. An almost identical pair without shackles is reproduced in *ibid.*, pl. 44.

12. Stuart Cary Welch, *A King's Book of Kings: the Shah-nameh of Shah Tahmasp*, New York, 1972, and *Persian Painting: Five Royal Safavid Manuscripts of the Sixteenth Century*, New York, 1976.

13. For two of the manuscripts made in Herat, see *ibid.*, pp. 55-61, and Peter J. Chelkowski and Priscilla P. Soucek, *Mirror of the Invisible World: Tales from the Khamseh of Nizami*, New York, 1975. There is also the *Divan* of Hafiz, executed in Herat in 1523, owned by the Freer Gallery of Art (32.45-32.54).

14. Two of the albums compiled by Shah Tahmasp and Bahram Mirza are in Istanbul, Topkapi Palace Museum, H. 2161 and H. 2154.

15. The manuscript (46.12) contains 28 illustrations (S. C. Welch, *Persian Painting*, pp. 98-127).

16. For studies of the art of Isfahan under Shah Abbas, see Ivan Stchoukine, *Les Peintures des Manuscrits de Shah Abbas Ier à la Fin des Safavis*, Paris, 1964, and Renata Holod (ed.), *Studies on Isfahan: Proceedings of the Isfahan Colloquium, Iranian Studies*, vol. VII (1974), 2 vols. See also the following two publications by Anthony Welch: *Shah Abbas and the Arts of Isfahan*, New York, 1973, and *Artists for the Shah: Late Sixteenth-Century Painting at the Imperial Court of Iran*, New Haven and London, 1976.

17. Friedrich Sarre and Eugene Mittwoch, *Zeichnungen von Riza Abbasi*, Munich, 1915, Abb. 4b.

18. A. U. Pope (ed.), *A Survey of Persian Art*, London and New York, 1964-65, vol. V, p. 1883.

19. Freer Gallery of Art, 33.7. Boston, Museum of Fine Arts, no. 14.368 (Ananda K. Coomaraswamy, *Les Miniatures Orientales de la Collection Goloubew au Museum of Fine Arts de Boston*, Paris and Brussels, 1929, no. 50, pl. XXVII).

20. Boston, Museum of Fine Arts, nos. 14.583-14.591 (*ibid.*, no. 43, pl. XXIII).

21. The paintings owned by Boston, Museum of Fine Arts, are published in *ibid.*, nos. 44-47, pls. XXII, XXIV-XXVI.

22. The dated drawing is in Paris, Louvre, no. 7111 (*L'Islam dans les Collections Nationales*, Edition de Musées Nationaux, Paris, 1977, no. 657). Muhammedi's drawings representing mystics and dervishes are in London, India Office Library, J.28.4 (B. W. Robinson, *Persian Paintings in the India Office Library*, London, 1976, no. 152, pl. V); Boston, Museum of Fine Arts, no. 14.649 (Coomaraswamy, *Les Miniatures Orientales*, no. 48, pl. XXVI); Leningrad, Hermitage (F. R. Martin, *The Miniature Painting and Painters of Persia, India and Turkey*, London, 1968, pl. 102); and in London, British Museum, formerly in a private collection (Thomas Arnold, *Painting in Islam*, New York, 1965, pl. XLVII).

23. The drawing with the kneeling youth is in Paris, Louvre, no. K 3427 (*L'Islam*, no. 659); the dervish is in Dublin, Chester Beatty Library, no. 242 (Anthony Welch, "Painting and Patronage under Shah Abbas I," *Studies on Isfahan*, pp. 458-507, fig. 2). Two other signed single-page paintings are in Istanbul, Topkapi Palace Museum, H. 2166, fol. 24b and H. 2156, fol. 45a (*ibid.*, pp. 460-463, fig. 1).

24. Also in Istanbul, Topkapi Palace Museum, H. 2166, fol. 18a (*ibid.*, fig. 3).

25. A drawing identical to no. 24 in the

exhibition was published in P & D Colnaghi & Co., Ltd., *Persian and Mughal Art,* London, 1976, no. 51.

26. Cl. Huart, *Les Calligraphes et les Miniaturistes de L'Orient Musulman,* Paris, 1908, p. 229.

27. Philipp Walter Schultz, *Die Persische-Islamische Miniaturmalerei,* Leipzig, 1914, vol. I, pp. 195 and 203.

28. Robinson, *Persian Painting,* no. 894.

29. Stchoukine, *Les Peintures de Manuscrits de Shah Abbas,* p. 61. The drawing with the signature is in Boston, Museum of Fine Arts, no. 14.638 (Coomaraswamy, *Les Miniatures Orientales,* no. 87, pl. XLIX), and the attributed example is in London, British Library (Titley, *Miniature from Persian Manuscripts,* no. 404-75).

30. Aka Riza was first identified with Riza-i Abbasi by Stchoukine in *Les Peintures des Manuscrits de Shah Abbas,* pp. 85-133.

31. Dublin, Chester Beatty Library, no. 277 (A. J. Arberry, B. W. Robinson, E. Blochet and J. V. S. Wilkinson, *The Chester Beatty Library: a Catalogue of Persian Manuscripts and Miniatures,* Dublin, 1962, vol. III, pp. 49-50).

32. The *Kisas al-Anbiya* is in Paris, Bibliothèque Nationale, suppl. pers. 1313 (A. Welch, "Painting and Patronage"); the *Divan* was formerly in the Rothschild Collection (Colnaghi, *Persian and Mughal Art,* no. 43); and the *Khosrau va Shirin* is in London, Victoria and Albert Museum (A. Welch, "Painting and Patronage").

33. *Ibid.,* pp. 62-72. One of the *Shahnames* is in two volumes: vol. I, dated 1634, is in Geneva, Prince Sadruddin Agha Khan Collection (A. Welch, *Shah Abbas and the Arts of Isfahan,* no. 57); vol. II, dated 1656, is in Dublin, Chester Beatty Library, no. 270 (*ibid.*). There is a second dispersed *Shahname,* dated 1648 (*ibid.,* no. 56; Colnaghi, *Persian and Mughal Art,* no. 55). A third copy of the same work, dated 1617, was illustrated by Muin ca. 1650-60 (Schultz, *Die Persische-Islamische Miniaturmalerei,* vol. II, pl. 169). The history of Shah Ismail, ca. 1650, is in London, British Library, Or. 3248 (Titley, *Miniatures from Persian Manuscripts,* no. 82). There are also several other *Shahnames* attributed to Muin; for instance, the two copies in London, India Office Library (Robinson, *Persian Paintings,* nos. 1083 and 1152). For more than 30 works assigned to this artist, see Ernst Kühnel, "Der Maler Muin," *Pantheon,* vol. 29, no. 5 (1942), pp. 108-114.

34. Sarre and Mittwoch, *Zeichnungen von Riza Abbasi.*

35. *Ibid.,* pls. 3B, 24, 25 and 39.

36. The Turkish painting (31 x 19.7 cm.) is in the Binney Collection (Binney, *Turkish Miniature Paintings,* no. 22). For the copy made in India (31.1 x 18.6 cm.), see Sotheby's *Fine Oriental Miniatures, Manuscripts and Qajar Paintings,* London, Tuesday, 4th April, 1978, no. 246.

37. The drawing was obtained from the Yildiz Palace by Sarre (Martin, *Miniature Paintings and Painters,* p. 33).

38. *Ibid.*

39. Each of the five books of this work has a colophon with the name of the scribe and the date and place of execution. Shah Mahmud's signature appears in the colophon of the fifth book, the *Subhat al-Abrar* (46.12, fol. 46a), which states that Shah Mahmud al-Nishapuri finished the work on October 6, 1556, in Meshhed (C. S. Welch, *Persian Painting,* pp. 98-127).

40. *Ibid.* Titley, *Miniatures from Persian Manuscripts,* pp. 71-97. Shah Mahmud worked on this manuscript between 1539 and 1543.

41. V. Minorsky, *Calligraphers and Painters: A Treatise by Qadi Ahmad, Son of Mir-Munshi,* Washington, D.C., 1959, pp. 135-138. The author of the treatise was Shah Mahmud's student and gives a detailed account of his master's life.

42. Ivan Stchoukine, *Les Peintures des Manuscrits Safavis de 1502 à 1587,* Paris, 1959, p. 43, and *Les Peintures des Manuscrits de Shah Abbas,* p. 73.

43. The figure here is drawn in the same pose but holds a book and pen. The size of this drawing is very close to that of the Freer example: 15.5 x 8.3 cm. (*L'Islam,* no. 659).

44. S. C. Welch, *A King's Book of Kings,* fol. 341v on pp. 165-167, and *Persian Painting,* pls. 39, 41, 46-48.

45. Richard Ettinghausen, "The Dance with Zoomorphic Masks and Other Forms of Entertainment Seen in Islamic Art," *Arabic and Islamic Studies in Honor of Hamilton A. R. Gibb,* ed. George Makdisi, Leiden, 1965, pp. 211-224.

46. Martin, *Miniature Painting and Painters,* pl. 102; Arnold, *Painting in Islam,* pl. XLVII. The unsigned version, dating from the early 17th century, is published in Richard Ettinghausen, "Stylistic Tendencies at the Time of Shah Abbas," *Studies on Isfahan,* pp. 593-628, fig. 6.

47. The only reference to this calligrapher appears in Georges Marteau and Henri Vever, *Miniatures Persanes,* Paris, 1913, "Signatures des Calligraphers," no. 36.

48. His signature appears on an album page in

Boston, Museum of Fine Arts, no. 14.562 (Coomaraswamy, *Les Miniatures Orientales,* no. 37a, pl. XIX).

49. The drawing was sold in 1976 (Colnaghi, *Persian and Mughal Art,* no. 51).

50. For recent publications on Mughal drawings and paintings with full references to related sources, see Stuart Cary Welch, *Indian Drawings and Painted Sketches,* New York, 1976, and *Imperial Mughal Painting,* New York, 1978; Milo Cleveland Beach, *The Grand Mogul: Imperial Painting in India 1600-1660,* Williamstown, Mass., 1978.

51. Pramod Chandra, *The Tuti-nama of the Cleveland Museum of Art,* Graz, 1976.

52. The project was conceived in 14 volumes, each with 100 paintings. It is thought to have been begun in 1550 by Humayun and been completed in 1580 by Akbar. The majority of the existing illustrations are in Vienna and published in facsimile in *Hamza-nama,* vol. I, Graz, 1974.

53. Four illustrated copies of the *Baburname* were made in the 1590s, all of which are incomplete and dispersed (Ellen Stevens Smart, *Paintings from the Baburnama: a Study of Sixteenth Century Mughal Historical Manuscript Illustrations,* University of London, 1977, doctoral dissertation). Three illustrated copies of the *Akbarname* were made during the lifetime of the subject (Deborah Brown Levine, *The Victoria and Albert Museum Akbar-nama: a Study in History, Myth and Image,* University of Michigan, 1974, doctoral dissertation published by University Microfilms, Ann Arbor, Michigan).

54. For the marginal drawings of this volume signed by Aka Riza and Daulat, see Yedda A. Godard, "Les Marges de Murakka Gulshan," *Athar-e Iran,* vol. I (1936), pp. 11-33.

55. Ernst Kühnel and Hermann Goetz, *Indische Buchmalereien aus dem Jahangir Album des Staatsbibliothek zu Berlin,* Berlin, 1924.

56. Milo Cleveland Beach, "The Gulshan Album and Its European Sources," *Bulletin of the Museum of Fine Arts,* Boston, vol. LXIII, no. 332 (1965), pp. 63-90.

57. Godard, "Les Marges du Murakka Gulshan," figs. 1-8.

58. The Freer Gallery of Art owns three paintings depicting Jahangir signed by this artist: 46.28, 48.28 (dated 1623) and 45.9 (Richard Ettinghausen, *Paintings of the Sultans and Emperors of India in American Collections,* New Delhi, 1961, pls. 11 and 12).

59. Huart, *Les Calligraphes,* p. 225. The name of this artist appears both in the Tehran and Berlin Jahangir albums. It is also found in the colophon of the *Khamsa* of Nizami, dated 1509,

in Dublin, Chester Beatty Library, no. 182
(Stchoukine, *Les Peintures des Manuscrits Safavis,*
no. 47); on an album leaf in London, India
Office Library, J. 28.5 (Robinson, *Persian
Paintings,* no. 222); and on a folio from an
Ottoman album in the Freer Gallery of Art,
33.6 (Esin Atil, *Turkish Art of the Ottoman
Period,* Washington, D.C., 1973, no. 5). The
style of Ali is almost identical to that of the
celebrated Mir Ali of Herat and both
calligraphers often use "al-Katib" and/or
"al-Sultani" after their name. It has been
suggested that the two names belong to the
same artist.

60. Minorsky, *Calligraphers and Painters,*
pp. 126-131. Many of his works are included in
the Tehran and Berlin Jahangir albums. The
Freer Gallery of Art owns several other Mughal
album leaves which contain Mir Ali's signed
examples: 07.258, 39.49, 39.50 and 48.28
(dated 1533-34).

61. For the works of Aka Riza, see Godard,
"Les Marges du Murakka Gulshan," figs. 1-8.
Govardhan's drawing is reproduced in Kühnel
and Goetz, *Indische Buchmalereien,* pl. 38.

62. For a detailed study of the *karg,* or
rhinoceros, see Richard Ettinghausen, *Studies in
Muslim Iconography: I. The Unicorn,*
Washington, D.C., 1950.

63. The most comprehensive study of this
school is in W. G. Archer, *Indian Paintings from
the Punjab Hills,* London, 1973, 2 vols.

64. *Ibid.,* vol. I, pp. 244-310; vol. II,
pp. 194-234.

65. This set is discussed in Alvan C. Eastman,
The Nala-Damayanti Drawings, Boston, 1959.

Appendix

Name of calligrapher	Cat. no.
Ali	62
Hasan Shamlu	21
Mir Ali (of Herat)	63, 64, 65
Mir Ali (of Tabriz)	1-7
Muhammed Huseyin al-Tabrizi	22
Muhammed Riza	15A
Shah Mahmud	12

Name of painter	Cat. no.
Abd al-Samad	65
Abu 'l-Hasan	68
Mirza Muhammed al-Huseyni	18
Muhammedi	15, 15A
Muhammed Muhsin	24, 25
Muin Musavvir	26, 34
Murad	15
Riza	19, 19A, 19B, 27-33
Sheykh Muhammed	16, 16A

Dated drawings	Cat. no.
1598	27
1613	18
1616	28
1619	35
1633	29
1638	30, 34, 36
1639	31, 33, 37, 38
1641	39, 40
1642	41, 42, 43
1643	44
1649	24
1672	26

Accession Numbers in Numerical Order

Acc. no.	Cat. no.	Acc. no.	Cat. no.
07.2	20	53.13	53
07.155	77	53.14	39
07.157	18	53.16	45
07.161	68	53.17	47
07.204	71	53.22	51
07.211	72	53.23	28
07.213	73	53.24	35
07.256	75	53.25	29
07.607	74	53.26	36
07.618	69	53.27	30
12.99	24	53.28	31
23.10	80	53.29	32
23.11	79	53.30	37
23.12	82	53.31	49
23.13	81	53.32	50
28.10	19	53.33	38
29.3	67	53.34	33
29.76	66	53.35	57
29.79	8	53.36	58
30.85	78	53.37	60
32.9	19A	53.39	40
32.30	1	53.40	48
32.31	2	53.41	41
32.32	3	53.42	55
32.33	4	53.43	52
32.34	5	53.44	42
32.35	6	53.45	43
32.37	7	53.46	46
37.8	15A	53.47	56
37.21	16A	53.48	44
37.23	16	53.49	59
37.25	10	53.57	34
38.14	9	53.58	54
40.18	17	54.24	19B
45.29	70	54.27	61
46.15	15	54.28	22
46.27	76	54.32	14
47.22	11	54.116	63
47.23	25	56.12	64
50.1	12	63.4	65
50.2	13	66.13	26
52.2	62	67.7	21
53.12	27	68.11	23

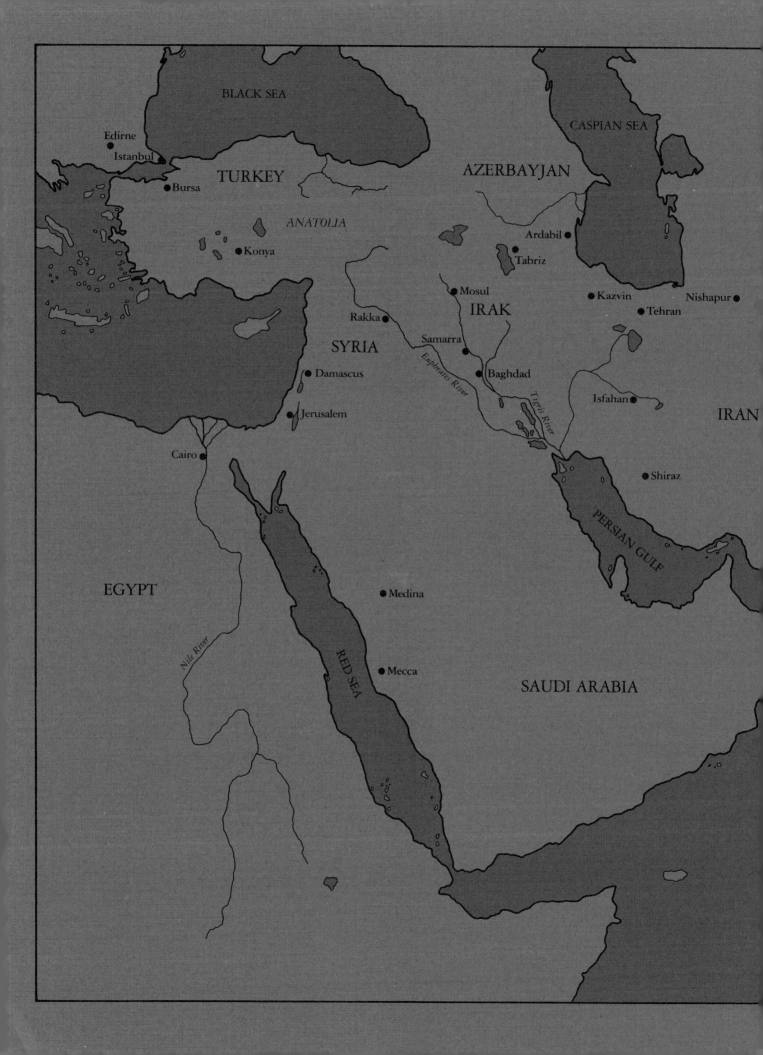

BLACK SEA

CASPIAN SEA

Edirne
Istanbul
Bursa

TURKEY

AZERBAYJAN

ANATOLIA

Konya

Ardabil

Tabriz

Mosul

Kazvin
Nishapur

IRAK

Tehran

Rakka

SYRIA

Samarra

Baghdad

Isfahan

IRAN

Damascus

Euphrates River

Tigris River

Jerusalem

Cairo

Shiraz

PERSIAN GULF

EGYPT

Nile River

Medina

RED SEA

Mecca

SAUDI ARABIA